BUMPING INTO GOD IN THE KITCHEN

Other Books by Fr. Dominic Grassi

Bumping into God

Bumping into God Again

Do You Love Me?

Living the Mass (with Joe Paprocki)

Still Called by Name

BUMPING INTO GOD IN THE KITCHEN

Savory Stories of Food, Family, and Faith

Fr. Dominic Grassi

LOYOLAPRESS.

CHICAGO

LOYOLAPRESS.

3441 N. ASHLAND AVENUE
CHICAGO, ILLINOIS 60657
(800) 621-1008
WWW.LOYOLABOOKS.ORG

All Scripture quotations are from the Jerusalem Bible, copyright © 1966, 1967, and 1968 by Darton, Longman & Todd, Ltd., and Doubleday, a division of Bantam Doubleday Dell, Inc. Reprinted by permission.

Cover and interior design by Rick Franklin

Library of Congress Cataloging-in-Publication Data
Grassi, Dominic.
  Bumping into God in the kitchen : savory stories of food, family, and faith / Dominic Grassi.
      p. cm.
  ISBN-13: 978-0-8294-1618-3
  ISBN-10: 0-8294-1618-8
  1. Food—Religious aspects—Christianity. 2. Dinners and dining—Religious aspects—Christianity. 3. Dinners and dining—Anecdotes.
4. Recipes. I. Title.
  BR115.N87G73 2007
  242—dc22

                                                      2006035393

Printed in the United States of America
07 08 09 10 11 12 Versa 10 9 8 7 6 5 4 3 2 1

To my family, in gratitude for all the meals that have come from their kitchens and all the love and stories and memories that we have shared around the table

A recipe is a story that ends with a good meal.

PAT CONROY

CONTENTS

ACKNOWLEDGMENTS

To George Lane, SJ—here it is, for better or worse, Loyola Press's first "cookbook" ever. Thank you for your belief in me. Terry Locke, you have supported me both as an author and as a priest, making me, I hope, better in both arenas of my life. Austin Tighe, you brought *Bumping into God* to life and changed my life because of it. Thank you.

Vinita Wright, you make my words say what I want them to say. And you have fed me at your table. What more can a writer ask of his editor? You have my gratitude and my respect.

Jim Manney, Matt Diener, and Tom McGrath: for all those lunches and subtle urgings to get the book done as I grew more and more introspective on my sabbatical, thanks. You knew that the way to my words was through my stomach.

And to Joe Durepos, know this: You came to me highly recommended as an agent. Then I found myself working for you at Loyola Press. And then you became my teacher with your incredible sabbatical reading list that kept me up until many a sunrise reading books I never would have taken off a shelf. Now I call you a friend. How does one thank another for that?

And I thank my brothers, whom I love dearly, not only for the recipes and the fodder for some of the stories, but also for allowing me to keep looking up to them. Yes, bros, I do, even if it gives you the occasional excuse to look down on your baby brother.

I finished writing this book while on sabbatical after eighteen years as pastor of St. Josaphat Parish in Chicago. That was the benchmark of my priesthood. To all the wonderful parishioners there, my profoundest and deepest thanks.

Finally, to all those who are part of my stories, written and unwritten, and to all those who have been and will be part of my life's recipes, I can only pray that these stories show you how grateful I am.

The sabbatical worked. I am ready for the next chapter.

INTRODUCTION

It is a story I love to tell. I use it quite often on talks that I give. I've used it in my writing many times And it fits so well here as an introduction to the third installment of my stories, reflections, and reminiscences, the first two called *Bumping into God* and *Bumping into God Again*. This one, as you ascertained from the cover, is entitled *Bumping into God in the Kitchen*. I know what you are thinking, so let me categorically state that there will not be future volumes dealing with various other rooms of the house. I could stretch and imagine *Bumping into God in the Laundry Room*. But the line has to be drawn somewhere. Still, why choose the kitchen as a focus for this group of stories?

A number of years ago, I gave a series of talks at a parish that was being formed by three parishes merging together. Breakfast was going to be served during the break after my first presentation. As I was speaking, tray after tray of bagels and donuts and sweet rolls were being set up behind those who were intently listening to me.

Bowls of fruit salad were carted in. Juice and coffee were brought out. After so many years of public speaking, I am amazed at how easily I can continue to talk while in my mind I am selecting my roll and what kind of cream cheese I want. The talk completed, I rushed to the back and made sure I got what I had mentally selected.

As I stood back up at the podium, enjoying the food I had rushed to get, a woman approached me. She had been taking copious notes during my talk. Even at this moment she had notebook and pen in hand, while everyone else was following my example at the food tables. She was well past middle age, and I guessed she had been very active in one of the three merging parishes. I smiled benignly at her, hoping there was no strawberry cream cheese stuck to my teeth.

She responded to my smile with a quick, business-like one of her own. "I just have an observation about your presentation," she stated. Before I could decide if the tone of her voice was friendly or hostile, she continued, "You sure do eat a lot in your parish." I wasn't sure if she was approving of the examples I had used, ranging from New Parishioners Dinners to Leadership Brunches to the Unity Ball and Dinner. I had also mentioned "hospitality in the park" after Masses, our International Dinner, and many other examples from the parish in which I was pastor at the time. A little unsure of myself, I simply responded, "They say a parish reflects its pastor." She gave me that same smile and walked back to her table and kept on writing. She never did go to the refreshment table.

Not only did the parish of St. Josaphat in Chicago reflect me, but clearly so has much of my writing over the years. As one woman said at a book signing for my second book, "Father, your stories always make me hungry!" I hope that at least some of that hunger is of a spiritual variety.

Yes, food has a dominant role in many of the stories I share, and thus in the books I write. That is part of my Italian heritage. Check my DNA and you'll find tomato sauce. One radio show I was on ended with the interviewer graciously comparing my books to the famous Chicken Soup series. I said with typical Italian bravado, "Who needs chicken soup when they can have lasagna?"

So in their wisdom, the great folks at Loyola Press decided *Why fight it?* and asked me to write a collection of stories more specifically about food and feasting. What makes this book different from the previous two is that food moves to center stage. Included are recipes for a complete Italian meal, from antipasto to *dolci* (or from beginning to end, for those of you not related to the Caesars).

Some of the recipes are classics that my mother made for decades. She passed them on through my brother

Tony, who sat her down in his own kitchen and had her walk him through the recipes. He would follow her instructions and then write them down. Other recipes in this book are versions of what she cooked that my brother Phil and his wife, Donna, and my brother Joe and I have adapted over the years. We seem to have inherited much from our mother, including our ability to cook in large quantities.

Our memories are often stirred by our senses—looking at a picture, smelling a flower, listening to music. For me—and, I venture to think, for many others—tasting certain foods again after many years, or even yesterday, can make moments that were special in our lives vivid again. These feasts or simple meals or coffee breaks shared with others become moments of grace, during which we bump into God and feel God's unconditional love in our lives. When shared, they become the stories of our lives. And when we share those stories over good food, generously served with love, we create yet more moments of grace and more stories to tell.

The writing of this book happened to coincide with the death of my mother and my departure after eighteen years from St. Josaphat Parish. Perhaps these events add a "bittersweet" flavor, which you will taste in some of these stories. But mourning is as much a part of life as celebrating and eating are. Sometimes all three can happen simultaneously. What I have come to realize is that we are who we are. We experience and deal with what life sends our way, with our own experiences of and faith in a loving God to help us through. Those blessings, like the memory of a loved one shared during a good meal, will never be taken away from us, especially if we continue to celebrate them by remembering them and sharing them.

These are my stories and recipes. I genuinely hope that they make you hungry, both spiritually and physically. If they do, try them out. Don't be a slave to them. Make them your own. I hope they will become catalysts for you to start sharing your recipes and your stories. Jesus himself chose the setting of a meal to say, "Do this in memory of me." A crucial aspect of our faith comes to us in the breaking of the bread. And so it is that we find ourselves bumping into God in the kitchen. It's as good a place as any, and better than most.

ANTIPASTO

You must make this pronouncement: . . .

"He brought us here and gave us this land, a land where milk and honey flow. Here then I bring the first fruits of the produce of the soil that you, Yahweh, have given me."

You must then lay them before Yahweh your God, and bow down in the sight of Yahweh your God. Then you are to feast on all the good things Yahweh has given you, you and your household, and with you the Levite and the stranger who lives among you.

DEUTERONOMY 26:5, 9–11

*A*ntipasto means "before the meal." Cold or hot, these foods were served to fill you up before the more expensive main courses were served. Cured meats, cheeses of all sorts, seasonal vegetables served raw or grilled, and preserved or pickled vegetables were part of this common fare. This ordinary stuff was made special by the creativity of the cook. Expanded menus today include salads that, at some tables, are eaten with the main courses or after them. Sometimes even a simple pizza or bread with seasoned oil is served prior to the main course.

A good antipasto selection can warm up not just the appetite but also the spirit, letting people know that they are welcome and that they won't have to hold back: there will be more than enough for everyone. Pour a glass of wine and pass the dishes—the stories will begin and become a part of the meal, as they should.

QUICK PICKLED PEPPERS

This is Mom's recipe that my brother adapted in order to fix the dish faster. My brother Phil serves it as an appetizer with crusty bread and chunks of Romano cheese or provolone. The peppers are also great on a sandwich with Genoa salami and mozzarella.

INGREDIENTS

1/2 cup light virgin olive oil

3 cloves garlic, halved

4 green bell peppers, cut in 1-by-2-inch pieces

1 red bell pepper, cut in 1-by-2-inch pieces

1 yellow or orange bell pepper, cut in 1-by-2-inch pieces

Salt and pepper

3/4 cup red wine vinegar mixed with 1/4 cup water

Fresh or dried basil

DIRECTIONS

Cover the bottom of a large frying pan with the olive oil and place over medium heat. Add the garlic cloves to the oil.

Decrease the heat to low and add the peppers, salt, pepper, and basil. Cover the pan.

Cook for 15 minutes for crispy peppers, or longer if you desire softer peppers, turning halfway through cooking.

Remove the peppers and place them in a bowl. Cover the bowl.

Pour out all but a tablespoon of the oil from the pan. Add the vinegar and water to the pan and bring to a boil; cook for 3 to 4 minutes.

Pour the heated vinegar and water over the peppers in the bowl, cover the bowl again, and refrigerate for a minimum of 2 hours, the longer the better.

Mom's Egg Balls

Warning: these can be addictive and can fill you up quickly. They are great served warm or at room temperature. Leftovers can be thrown into your tomato sauce and served with pasta. Too much baking powder will create a monster; too little, and the egg balls will be flat and heavy. Two of my nieces have become pros in egg ball cooking. A tradition lives on.

Ingredients

12 eggs

1 cup milk

1 cup breadcrumbs

1/2 cup grated Romano cheese

Salt and pepper

Fresh or dried basil

Garlic powder

1 cup all-purpose flour

Corn oil

1/3 cup olive oil

2 teaspoons baking powder

DIRECTIONS

Whisk together the eggs and the milk, then add the breadcrumbs and the Romano cheese.

Add salt, pepper, basil, and garlic powder to taste, then slowly add the flour. Let the mixture sit for 15 minutes.

Heat 2 inches of corn oil in a frying pan over medium heat or in an electric skillet. Carefully sprinkle the olive oil on top of the slowly heating corn oil.

Add the baking powder to the batter and mix again.

Spoon one of the balls of batter into the hot oil, turning until golden brown. Adjust the heat and the seasonings if necessary. Fry the remaining balls of batter. Place the fried egg balls on paper towels to soak up excess oil.

Serve immediately.

MY OWN
SAUSAGE AND PEPPERS

I created this dish using ingredients I like; that's the fun of cooking. This dish can be made ahead and reheated in the microwave. Add whatever ingredients you like, or modify those given here. This dish goes well with crostini or Italian breadsticks, and leftovers can be served in warm Italian bread, cut lengthwise and hollowed out.

INGREDIENTS

2 pounds sweet Italian sausage, cut into 1-inch cubes

1 pound hot Italian sausage, cut into 1-inch cubes

3 cloves garlic, minced

2 green bell peppers, julienned

1 red or orange bell pepper, julienned

1 yellow bell pepper, julienned

2 large sweet onions, sliced

1 small jalapeño pepper, diced

Salt and pepper

Balsamic vinegar

DIRECTIONS

Fry the sausage in a large frying pan over high heat until cooked. Remove the sausage, leaving the fat in the pan, and drain on paper towels.

Add the garlic, the peppers, the onions, and the jalapeño pepper to the fat in the pan. Add salt and pepper to taste.

Cook ingredients until they just start to soften and then return the sausage to the pan.

Immediately add enough vinegar to cover all the ingredients.

Cover the pan with a lid, decrease the heat, and simmer until the onions start to get limp.

Serve immediately or refrigerate and reheat.

My Own Tomato-and-Bread Salad

Italians have always found creative ways to use leftover bread. Here is mine. This is a simple and quick dish that can even be a light summer lunch. Keep in mind that too much liquid will make the bread soggy. Mixing the two vinegars gives the dish both a sweet and a tart taste. Add a little lemon juice, crumbled Gorgonzola cheese, and toasted pine nuts, and the dish becomes more of a meal. Toast the bread in the oven and rub it with garlic for a different taste. Adapt, add, change. Make it your own.

Ingredients

5 or 6 ripe tomatoes, coarsely chopped

1 sweet onion, thinly sliced

4 or 5 fresh sweet basil leaves, torn into pieces

Stale Italian bread, cubed, enough to almost fill the bowl used for serving

Extra virgin olive oil

Balsamic vinegar

Red wine vinegar

Salt and pepper

DIRECTIONS

Combine the tomatoes, the onion, the basil leaves, and half of the bread in a bowl.

In a separate bowl, mix equal parts olive oil, balsamic vinegar, and red wine vinegar. Pour the mixture into the bowl with the tomatoes while mixing the ingredients, leaving a trace of dressing at the bottom of the bowl. Add more bread as you like.

Add salt and pepper to taste. Mix again. Refrigerate and serve cold.

1

SUNDAY PASTA

*M*ost family meals were important when I was growing up. But unlike the families we saw on the television shows *Father Knows Best* and *Leave It to Beaver*, we didn't gather for a big family dinner every night. Mom would feed her four sons, or any of us who were home, sometime around six o'clock. When she finished with us, she would get a meal ready for Dad, who arrived home from the grocery store around seven thirty— and much later on Fridays, when the store remained open until nine. She would always eat with him.

Even though we did not all eat together during the week, our evenings had a definite routine. First of all, Dad did not want us to watch television before he arrived home from work. It seemed to us kids that he didn't want us to enjoy the television if he couldn't, but it probably had more to do with his perception that the old RCA console TV consumed a lot of electricity and our watching it would hike the utility bill. So we made sure to turn off the set early enough so that the tubes would cool down before Dad got home, in case he decided to check on us by touching the top of the set.

Another part of our routine involved the chain-link fence that surrounded our backyard and the parking area. It had a double-wide gate, and whenever it was opened, a piece of metal on the bottom of it dragged on the ground, producing a scraping sound that could be heard in the house. Dad saw it as our duty to make certain the gate was open when he came home from work; this would save him the trouble of getting out of the car to do it. At the same time, he didn't want the gate open too early, because he liked our yard to be secure.

I can remember the feelings of dread that would come over my brothers and me when, on occasion, we lost track of time and our illegal TV-watching was interrupted by the sound of that back gate scraping open. Dad would storm into the house, mad because he'd had to get out of the car to open the gate. Then he would check the television set and find it still warm.

Another evening routine developed that, as far as I can remember, involved only Dad and me when I was little. Given the right circumstances—which included the gate being open at the right time and the top of the television being cool—I would sit on Dad's lap and look at his big hands. Surprisingly, they were not very calloused, even though he had done physical labor his whole life. My mother would say his hands were soft, like a baby's. She told me that I had inherited my hands from him. Embedded in the skin of the fingers of his right hand were small flecks of metal. He told me that they were reminders of his years working in the coal mines of Pennsylvania. This fascinated me. I can't count the number of times I asked him if those pieces of metal hurt. He would chuckle and say, "Not at all," and I would press on them in awe.

When I grew too old to sit on Dad's lap, he would call me over to his chair before he sat down for dinner and say, "Dominic, loosen my shoes." I would sit on the floor in front of him and untie the laces of his high-top work shoes until he would sigh with satisfaction. The truth is I didn't mind this special task—he never asked my brothers, only me—until I was older and occasionally my friends would be present when Dad asked me to loosen his shoes. Out of the corner of my eye, I could see them trying to hide a smile, and it embarrassed me.

After Dad finished eating dinner, he'd watch a little TV. He liked the fights, Perry Como (because he was Italian), and the news. He was in bed by ten thirty. I never saw him read a book or even the *Chicago Tribune*, which was delivered daily. He never talked to us about his day or asked us about ours. This was pretty much our weeknight routine.

It was precisely this routine that made Sunday pasta so special. On Sundays after Mass, everyone was expected to be around the kitchen table. (The dining room was reserved strictly for holidays.) The choice of noodle would change—one week it would be rigatoni, the next week ziti—but the tomato sauce would always be the one Mom cooked for hours on Saturday. The table would be set with the free Watt Pottery terra-cotta dishes given out by the R&F Spaghetti Company, which are now worth hundreds of dollars to collectors.

Cucumbers sliced into spears, sharp-tasting red radishes, and crisp celery stalks sat in bowls, giving off a fresh, earthy smell. Steaming bowls of pasta covered with the rich sauce and optional grated Romano or dry ricotta cheese were placed in front of everyone. A big bowl of meat that had been cooked in the sauce awaited us in the center of the table. This dish included meatballs, rolled and stuffed flank steak, neck bones, oxtails, lamb ribs, and occasionally pig's feet, but we could not eat the meat until we had finished our pasta. A loaf or two of Gonnella twist bread was passed around, from which we would break off a piece to "spoonce in the soak," which means "dunk in the sauce." We drank Canada Dry Ginger Ale colored with a splash of dollar-a-gallon Petri Wine. Too much ginger ale would draw a look from Dad. He was always conscious of the food Mom took from the store to feed the family.

It was during this Sunday meal that we talked as a family, though I confess I don't remember what we talked about. But I do remember lots of laughter. On Sundays, Dad was usually more relaxed and less tired than during the week. After lunch, Mom did the dishes. Dad napped. My brothers and I went off to entertain ourselves.

Sunday pasta offered us great comfort. We knew exactly what to expect, what we would see, smell, taste, hear, and feel. When I was feeling insecure as a child, the Sunday pasta routine calmed me and reminded me that everything would be just fine. I was safe, surrounded by my family and by the comforting smells and tastes that were so much a part of me that I could not put into words how much I craved them. There at the table, my past heritage and my present family pointed me toward a future with a potential I am still trying to appreciate. Around that table I learned the trust and the love that would bring me to where I am today.

When I went off to seminary, the Sunday lunch was grand, with ham or roast beef or fried chicken. But I was never quite as hungry as I had been during those years before, because it wasn't Sunday pasta around the kitchen table with the family. Only now, decades later, do I realize that what I hungered for was not so much the food as the spiritual nourishment the Sunday pasta represented. I think this understanding has made me a better priest, as I share God's love around Jesus' table with all who come. I want them to feel as safe and as loved as I did with my family when we shared Sunday pasta.

2

COMMON SENSES

*V*ery often when I give talks or conduct retreats or make presentations, or after someone has read one of my books, I am asked, "How do you remember all those stories with such detail?" At first I didn't have an answer. Over time, however, I grew to realize what triggered my memories. And so now I respond, "It's just common senses, that's all." Usually a story or a memory comes back to me or into clearer focus because of something I detect with one or more of my senses. The more I concentrate on what I am smelling or hearing or seeing or tasting, the clearer the memory and the more detailed the story. Here are some examples.

I dislike the smell of roses, whether the flowers themselves or in perfume. That strong, sweet smell, so rich it almost takes my breath away, reminds me of my grandfather's funeral, when I was seven years old. Suddenly I am standing once again in front of that stiff and altogether frightening body. I remember fearing that he would sit up and look at me. I can still see all the flowers around the coffin, most of them roses. The funeral parlor was too hot, and that thick scent almost made me swoon. I looked away from the corpse and saw another bouquet of roses around a clock face that indicated the time of death. Ever since, I have seen stopped clocks as bad luck for me, as harbingers of death. Roses at a wedding or on a dining room table or in a vase carry me back to that night, and each time I remember more details.

Even touch can jog my memory. I can't wear bulky sweaters of material that scratches my arms or neck. That feeling reminds me of a camel hair coat I wore when I was eight years old. It was a hand-me-down from one or two of my older brothers. The collar was frayed and scratched my neck. The lining in the sleeves was gone, and my arms itched and itched. Because the coat had no buttons by the time I got it, Mom would secure it with safety pins, so it was both uncomfortable and embarrassing to wear. I felt like a war orphan from the comic strips. Today, if my neck or arms itch from what I am wearing, I feel that everyone is laughing at me.

Sometimes, hearing something can bring some long-ago experience rushing back. I don't hear the old Western song "Red River Valley" much anymore, which is fortunate.

When I was twelve, someone gave me a yellow LP of cowboy songs. It was the first LP I owned, and I thought it was pretty neat. My older brothers had their Elvis albums, and my parents had their Robert Alda (he was the father of the actor Alan Alda and sounded like Perry Como). And now I had my own record, which I played one Saturday morning, over and over on our De Forest TV/stereo console. Just as Gene Autry was singing, "Do not hasten to bid me adieu" to some pretty cowgirl who was leaving him, my brother Joe came downstairs and broke the record in half without saying a word. I went numb, and that feeling returns when I hear that song. But I also remember sneaking up to Joe's room after that when he wasn't there and scratching some of his records and tearing random pages from his art books. I wonder if he remembers any of that.

Not all the memories are negative. I can't help but grin when I see a picture of the Washington Monument. I remember standing in front of it during my senior class trip, the trip on which I'd flown on an airplane for the first time. My friends and I were looking at the Washington Monument when one of our teachers announced— he'd just gotten word—that I had won second place in a national contest for yearbook writing. My career as a writer had begun. I felt grown up and successful. Now when I get writer's block, I just pull out a picture of the monument and I can write again.

You probably already suspect that my most heightened sense is taste. Food plays an important role in my life, and I know that much of the joy I get from food is connected to memory. That moment when raw ingredients are transformed into a genuine tomato sauce thickening and simmering on the stove is special to me. Mom would not let me dunk bread into sauce that had already been cooking for a couple of hours: she feared the crumbs might sour her sauce, which still had a ways to go. So I waited for her okay. When it was time, what I got was not just a taste of that rich tomato sauce. It was a feast for all my senses: I tasted, smelled, felt, saw, and even heard, in the bubbling sauce, all of Mom's love, all the safety and protection of our warm kitchen and what it meant to be home. I can barely begin to capture in words what I was feeling.

Pay attention to your senses, and they will bring back vivid memories. It is no wonder that the sacramental moments Jesus left for us involve our senses in one way or another. We eat the bread and we drink from the cup. We see and we smell and we feel the oil that anoints us and heals us. We hear the word of God from each other and from the deacon or the priest or the bishop. We embrace each other with Christ's peace. Our senses hold on to and bring back a tradition and heritage containing memories and stories that go back more than two thousand years. Our sensory memories pay homage to those sacred moments in which God comes to us.

3

DANDELION WINE

One day early in spring, I saw an elderly lady with a knife clipping dandelion shoots on an embankment along the expressway. I had to stop and ask, using an old dialect, if she was gathering dandelions. She was surprised that I knew and had used the right words. We chatted, and memories flooded back to me.

Early in life, I learned an important lesson: food that seems strange to one person might very well be a delicacy for another. I am thinking specifically of the dandelion, which we call a weed, known as *cataloine* in the dialect spoken by Italians from the southern hills of Bari. It is the bane of manicured lawns in America. But did you know it was brought here to be cultivated as a delicacy? When it went to flower in gardens, its seed blew wild, and it became almost impossible to eliminate because of its deep roots and its ability to survive on little water.

My family brought many peasant customs with them to America. But they were not nourished by the new, urban environment, any more than tomatoes or peppers can grow from seed scattered on cement sidewalks. Many of these customs faded, but like tenacious weeds, some traditions and ways of doing things clung to life, finding ways to take root. Such was the case with the wild dandelions and how they were gathered and used in our kitchen.

Forget about the broad-leaved plant with yellow flowers that during mid- and late summer takes over backyards as well as front lawns, and parks, and sides of expressways—wherever grass is trying to grow. By then it is useless, unless you take the yellow flowers and let them ferment into golden dandelion wine.

The right time to pick dandelions is during those weeks just before spring blooms into colors and scents seemingly overnight—that pregnant time when most of the ground is brown and muddy after winter's ice and slush have melted away. It is then that the first shoots of dandelions will pop out, before anything else, even before the buds on the trees and the tulips. The dandelion shoots appear tiny and scrawny, with tender leaves such a deep green that they look almost gray.

When I was too young to attend school, I would go with Mom and Nona and Aunt Mary when they sought the dandelions. They would bundle me up and put on their babushkas and sweaters to ward off the early-morning chill. Each would be armed with a paring knife and four folded shopping bags. The four of us would go to Lincoln Park, because the women in my family preferred the sloping terraces along the side of Lake Shore Drive. I wasn't very happy to be with them. There was nothing for me to do but sit on the damp ground and watch.

The three of them were stocky, their legs so short that getting down on their knees gave them no advantage in picking the dandelions. So, standing stiff-legged, they would reach down and with one swift, clean motion chop off the dandelion just below ground level so the leaves would stay intact on the plant. When my mother, grand-mother, and aunt bent over, their substantial backsides went up in the air, and they shook with the rhythm of the motion as they scooped dandelion after dandelion from the damp soil. I am sure it appeared to many motorists on their way downtown to work that some ancient ritual dance was taking place on the side of the road.

After a few hours, large bunches of harvested dandeli-ons would bulge out of the shopping bags, which proudly proclaimed Ben Adamowski for state's attorney. He sure gave out a lot of shopping bags. Years later, he ran for mayor and lost, but I can remember senior citizens walking down the street with either one of his bags or one from Goldblatt's Department Store, or both. My family was not political, but they did need a lot of bags when the dandelions were in season.

By midmorning, we were home. The kitchen took on a damp, earthy smell, brought in with the plants and their formerly dirt-bound roots. The women washed the dandelions in ice-cold water in the sink and then rinsed and washed them again, trimming them until they looked quite elegant. Some of the plants were destined for the big pot of boiling water on the stove, where they would be cooked very much like spinach and served lightly oiled and salted as a side dish. Some were served uncooked as a salad, mixed with garlic, infused red wine vinegar, olive oil, and salt and pepper. Others would be boiled along with whole-wheat orecchiette pasta and then tossed with garlic, olive oil, and grated Romano cheese. But the best use of the dandelion greens was to mix them in with cooked, mashed fava beans. A dried fava bean looks like someone's big toe. The beans had to be shelled, boiled, and then mashed. Olive oil was stirred in, along with chunks of stale Italian bread and handfuls of dandelion greens, creating a most unique dish. The beans have the starchy consistency of mashed potatoes and pick up the rich taste of the olive oil and the earthy bitter flavor of the greens.

As much as I complained about going to the park with the women on these picking expeditions, I enjoyed all the different dishes that were the outcome of their labors. I miss those special tastes now. There is no way to replicate them. I am not about to go to the park with a knife (I'd get arrested) and a shopping bag. And seeing all the dogs running around the park and the pesticides and fertilizers being used now makes me less eager to eat the dandelions.

But I'll never be able to look upon dandelions as weeds. They are a much-maligned, overlooked food, soon to be lost. These recipes could very well disappear, and with them the peasant wisdom that found nourishment in what the rest of us ignore or eradicate. Discovered out of hunger and poverty, dandelions and other wild plants became delicacies and fed generations, much like the simple, trusting faith of those before us nourished their souls. I pray that we don't forget our roots and lose what feeds our souls as we grow more sophisticated and worldly in our tastes. That's why I was so happy to discover the woman on the side of the expressway doing what my family did fifty years ago.

4

COMFORT FOOD

*M*ost of us can identify our comfort food. For any number of reasons it serves to calm us or at least help us in some small way through a difficult day or week. Sometimes it's easier to name our comfort food than it is to explain how it became such a powerful force for us.

I can trace the origins of my comfort food to a snowy evening way back in 1955, when I was in the second grade. The sisters and the priests of Our Lady of Mt. Carmel School decided to stage a "vocation cavalcade." That meant dressing up lots of clueless children in the medieval habits of the different religious communities and orders. In this decade before Vatican Council II, traditional habits were still being worn. Dressed in these habits, students would present a memorized history of the group they were dressed to look like. This would be done at an assembly to which the whole parish was invited.

There were little seven-year-old girls dressed like "God's geese," as the Daughters of Charity were called. Others wore what looked like little valentine hearts around their heads, representing the Sisters of Christian Charity. There were Franciscans, Dominicans, Sisters of the Holy Family of Nazareth, and Felicians (which does not rhyme with *pelicans*, we were told). But the two girls who were dressed like miniature Sisters of Mercy, with starched linen bibs, leg-length rosaries, and black leather belts, received a standing ovation. Those were *our* sisters. They deserved the accolades. I am profoundly grateful for the great education they gave me. Decades later I became convinced that George Lucas had stolen their habit and put it on Darth Vader.

The boys didn't have such exotic garb, with the exception of the Franciscans and the Dominicans. Most of us were dressed in some variation of the black cassock, some with special hoods or collars or crosses or emblems. A classmate and I were told that we had been given the highest honor: we had been selected to represent the diocesan priests who served most of the parishes in Chicago. That meant we wore a simple black cassock and a black biretta with a puffy black ball on top. This was a much better outfit than the one I had worn as a page boy at the May Crowning two years earlier—powder blue shorts, a silk T-shirt, and a beret with a long blue feather. A picture from that ceremony shows an excruciatingly embarrassed five-year-old.

All the participants in the vocations cavalcade came out in pairs. But only one in each pair had to make a presentation. Not only was I the one in my pair to speak, but I was also the last of the speakers, the grand finale of the show. That meant I had time to grow more and more nervous as the evening wore on and as I listened to classmates who had been perfect in rehearsal now flub their lines or fall silent with panic or, in the case of the seven-year-old Carmelite, run unceremoniously from the stage. The sisters looked mortified even though the audience oohed and aahed and was forgiving of the imperfections. Meanwhile, I was a mess.

Finally, my moment arrived. I walked out with my partner. I looked out and saw my mother smiling reassuringly and my dad rushing up the aisle to his seat. He had just closed the grocery store. The look that Mom gave him as he sat down made it clear that it was good he'd at least made it in time for my performance. Seeing Dad made me even more nervous.

But I surprised myself. The words came out in the right order, loud enough, and just barely slow enough. I started to relax. But when I trumpeted proudly that after attending Quigley Prep, those continuing their studies for the priesthood would go to St. Mary of the Lake Cemetery, the laughter started, and it continued as I finished, bowed, and walked off. I didn't know the difference between a cemetery and a seminary. (Even today I'm not sure.) As the lights came on and people put on their coats, I was sure they were still laughing at me.

I went back to the classroom, took off the cassock, and froze. I could not go out and face the people. So I ran into the boys' bathroom and stayed there despite the urinals that flushed automatically every three minutes, scaring me every three minutes.

Before long, I heard my mother's voice. Dad had grown tired of waiting and had gone home, knowing it would be a late dinner. When I didn't answer her, Mom did the unspeakable and came into the boys' bathroom. The sisters were the only women allowed in. Mom's smile only brought on my tears. "Come on," she said. "Let's go. I'm so proud of you." She held out her hand. But I wouldn't budge. She kept smiling. "I know what we'll do," she said, and then she uttered the words that made all the difference then and that I still say to myself today when I am feeling defeated: "We'll go for a hot fudge sundae." Suddenly I was smiling even with the tears still in my eyes. I know this because right then she snapped a picture of me with her Kodak Brownie camera, and I still have that picture.

It would be no ordinary hot fudge sundae. It may have looked as if Mr. Berger made it at the pharmacy soda fountain with Borden's ice cream, but it tasted as if the angels themselves had made it. This is why hot fudge sundaes have become my comfort food. I save them for special moments when I need them most.

A few years back I gave a series of Lenten talks to a parish in a far northern suburb. I was hurting because my friend Jack had died. We had attended school together, been ordained together, and shared ministry. His burial occurred on the day my Lenten talks began, and some in the congregation knew of my sadness. After my last talk, the congregation invited me to go out with them. It was late, and I wasn't in the mood. But I accepted the invitation.

In my opening talk I had shared the story of the hot fudge sundae, explaining how that treat had become for me a metaphor of how God's grace heals us. So imagine my delight when I walked into the restaurant to find twenty-five tables occupied by people who had attended the Lenten talks, each person lifting a hot fudge sundae in the air as a supportive toast. As they handed me a double sundae, I could not help but feel God's grace working in me as it had years before. It's amazing what comfort food can do for the soul.

5

PIZZA DAY

*T*he day would begin with a large pan of boiled Idaho potatoes cooling just inside the screen door by the stairs above the kitchen. The first floor of our house was called an English basement; to go outside from there we had to go up five steps. At the top of the steps was where Mom put the potatoes to cool, early in the morning before we left for school. The potatoes were the welcome sign that it was "pizza day," because Mom's pizza (and homemade bread) started with potato-based dough.

My brothers and I were among the few students at our school who did not eat lunch in the cafeteria. We'd go home for lunch, and on pizza day a variety of delicious aromas would pleasantly assault our senses when we walked in the door. The potatoes from that morning would have been transformed into thick dough. Mom used a large tin laundry tub for this task. In it she would knead pounds of dough, the yeasty stuff engulfing her arms up to the elbows. As soon as we walked in the door, she would nod to us to get our sandwiches from the refrigerator. While we ate our lunch, she would continue kneading the dough, at intervals sprinkling it (and herself) with flour. The yeast gave off an intoxicating, alcoholic scent, and that aroma mingled in the air with the odors coming from the pots on the stove. One contained the tomato sauce that would cover most of the pizzas. Another was filled with onions and olives and other ingredients that would fill the stuffed pizzas—true pizza pies.

With everything smelling so good, we hated to leave for afternoon classes. But we knew what awaited us when we rushed home from school, skipping the altar servers' practice or the fast-pitching game or anything else that would normally keep us around the church or the schoolyard for hours.

When we reached that screen door, we were met by the smell of bread baking in the oven. We'd wait anxiously until Mom told us it was ready; then we'd each grab a stick of butter from the refrigerator, take one of the small loaves baked just for us, tear it open, and cover the bread with butter that instantly melted from the steaming heat. That was as close as we could ever get to eating manna from heaven.

Mom knew what she was doing. Our hunger now satisfied for a while, we'd do our homework or go out to play without bugging her for a taste of the pizzas, which she would soon place on both racks in her oven. Pizza was our dinner, plain and simple—no side dishes, no soup, no salad. It was pizza and milk or, if we were lucky, pizza and ginger ale. We would each get one slice of the stuffed pizza pie, with the onions and olives and sliced meatballs falling out of the baked crusts, and as many slices as we wanted of the simple yet delicious red-sauce-and-cheese-covered pizza.

When we finished eating, Mom would line us up. There would be a pizza to take to Mrs. LaFrance, in the boardinghouse near the church; another to take to the Durbin family, across the alley; and others to whomever else was on her list.

When we returned home from these errands, it would be time to open the back gate so that Dad could park the Chrysler when he came home from work. He and Mom would sit down to the last of the pizza and bread, which she had put aside for them. And they would eat it together when her stomach, afflicted by an ulcer, would allow her to join in.

Then Mom would get to the dishes, pots, and pans, washing and cleaning until nearly eight thirty, before joining us in the living room to watch a little television. She would look totally exhausted. Even as a child I thought she seemed so small compared to the other mothers. How could so much great food come from such a little person?

Much to our disappointment, there were never any leftovers on pizza day. We always seemed to have to take what was left to some other person or family. What began before dawn with the simple boiling of potatoes ended well after dark, with all the pizza gone, gone until the next pizza day a few months later, when there by the screen door would be the telltale pan of cooling boiled potatoes.

Years ago, my brother Tony finally convinced our mother to walk him through her recipes for her pizzas, with their sauces and fillings. Now he will occasionally cook them as part of a special meal. Everything tastes wonderful. And I am most appreciative of his preserving the recipes and a little bit of those memories for all of us.

As a priest, every day I break bread and pray, "Do this in memory of me." My brother bakes the wonderful bread that becomes the pizza that we share in memory of Mom. As good as it is, and as much as it brings back memories of her, it is not quite the same. Some days I just miss Mom, and her pizza, so much. Does the bread I break and pray over and share every day even come close to what Jesus gave his disciples on that first Holy Thursday? I know that as a priest I am supposed to say yes, and on a good day, I do—with confidence. But I wonder what we, in our humanness and our poor memory, miss of our feast with God, even on a good day.

6

THE GUEST LIST

*F*or a variety of reasons my parents had a very small
wedding, and there weren't a lot of pictures taken
to commemorate the event. So when it came time for
their twenty-fifth wedding anniversary, my brothers and
I decided to throw them a real celebration in the old-
fashioned Italian way. This would prove to be no small
task, because Joe and Phil were in college, and Tony and
I were still in high school.

We got Mom and Dad's approval, selected the date,
put a deposit on the Knickerbocker Hotel off Michigan
Avenue in Chicago, and hired a band. We asked our folks
to put together a list of guests, and then we joined their
list with ours. Our goal was to make it both a family and
a neighborhood celebration. We didn't realize then that
the cost of it would require each of us to work two sum-
mers at the family grocery store. But we knew it would be
worth whatever it took.

We had relatives coming from all over the country, and most of them would be eating and sleeping at our house the nights before, during, and after the celebration. Our guest list included the employees of the grocery store, our doctor and lawyer, our neighbors, the parishioners, and Sam the barber. We selected the Knickerbocker not only because it had a transparent dance floor that changed colors decades before disco was invented, but also because it served an ample ham dinner at a price we could afford for the two hundred guests who had accepted the invitation. It wouldn't be the Italian feast we had hoped for, but no one would go home hungry.

It was a memorable night in many ways. I had always been accused of having two left feet, but I started the night out with two actual left shoes. Yes, for some inexplicable reason, the box I came home with from the shoe store contained two left shoes. I had to wear an old, hastily polished pair with my first-ever tuxedo. Mr. Glow, who owned the shoe store, was at the party and was mortified when he found out about it.

My brother Phil, who had just broken up with his girl-friend, stunned the crowd with his date. Mary Candice was one of his former classmates from Our Lady of Mt. Carmel School and had since become—if only the good Sisters of Mercy knew—a Playboy Bunny. She made it into more pictures than I did. But I was grateful to my brother, not only for bringing someone so attractive to look at but also for telling the bartenders to serve me anything I wanted, since I was helping pay for the evening. Consequently, I don't remember much of what happened after ten.

But I do remember the pastor of the parish, Fr. Tom Byrne, giving my parents a splendid, if Irish, toast and leading all of us in singing "Let Me Call You Sweetheart," which I suppose was an infinitely better choice than a truly Italian tune such as "Lazy Mary." My brother Joe's simple toast to the "two greatest parents in the world" said it all, even if it came from the person least expected to say those words. Being the oldest, he was a bit of a rebel and fought a lot with our parents. It was indeed a night of surprises.

The next day, the house was filled with faux silver trays and candlesticks and one real silver-plated gift, from good old Dr. Del Chicca and his wife. Between the gifts and the relatives sleeping it off late into the morning, there wasn't much room to move around in the house. So I wandered up to the corner drugstore to rehydrate myself with a chocolate phosphate before returning one of the left shoes for a proper right one.

Mr. Berger, the pharmacist, told me that he had heard about the party and asked me how it went. Mr. Berger had brought medicine directly to the house when my grandfather was ill. He always put extra hot fudge on my sundaes. He didn't yell at me when I'd sneak a peek at the adult magazines in the rack. And Mr. Berger was the one neighbor and shopkeeper we had forgotten to invite. His wife stiffened and walked away before I could answer his question. Even then, as young as I was, I sensed that we had done something horribly wrong.

Mr. and Mrs. Berger were Jewish and childless. We had probably overlooked them because they weren't part of our family or church communities. Our barber, Sam, also childless, was an usher at our church, so we had remembered him. But the Bergers hadn't made it onto our guest list.

After that I could never bring myself to order a hot fudge sundae from the drugstore soda fountain, and when Tastee Freez opened up across the street, Mr. Berger took out the fountain and added more medicines.

One of us should have thought to invite them. It is hard to admit, even four decades later, that maybe our own prejudices and those of our society prevented us from seeing the Bergers as our neighbors. How easy it is to leave out those who are even a little different from us. Maybe we would have included them if they had had children who were our playmates in the neighborhood.

Who knows? What a shame that they weren't present. A hearty mazel tov would have been as much of a blessing as the Irish toast or the Italian salute or any of the other congratulations offered to my parents that night.

So I offer to you, Mr. and Mrs. Berger, a belated but sincere apology. We should have invited you—and we should have had something other than ham to serve you. It would have been a privilege to break bread with you. You were good and generous neighbors to us and to so many other customers of your drugstore at Briar and Broadway.

I try hard now to make sure that no one is left out of any celebration. For example, when a formal ball was instituted at St. Josaphat Parish, I was conscious of those who could not afford the tickets along with the formal clothing, downtown parking fees, and babysitters. A parish party needs to be for all parishioners. So we always set aside seats donated by folks who could not attend for any parishioners who wanted to come but could not afford it. I would have it no other way.

7

THE
"ORDEAL OF FOOD"

*E*very family should have traditions that link them to their past and to their heritage, but also traditions that are unique to themselves. The same is true with our family of faith. We find God's loving presence in similar ways, but also in ways that are ours alone.

One of my family's great traditions was the holiday meal. My brother has carousel after carousel of 35 mm slides documenting our holidays, birthdays, graduations, and more, but, now close to half a century old, they have started to fade. We take them out only about once every decade, possibly because they have become a little unsettling to look at. Mom and Dad are younger in those pictures than my brothers and I are now.

The holiday slides are pretty much the same from year to year. The old home on Briar Place might be decorated differently or have a different configuration of tables, according to the number of people Mom was expecting for the meal. But one thing remained constant: how absolutely exhausted she looked.

Ours was an all-male household except for her. My father, brothers, and I did not cook. We did not clean or do the wash. We did not even make our own beds. In those days we considered all of that women's work, a thought that is appalling to me now. Mom did it all, including cooking for twenty-plus people on holidays. The preparations often would begin a full week before the meal. She would be up the entire night before roasting the turkey.

Holiday meals were quite elaborate, going well beyond the bounty of Sunday pasta. Inevitably, we witnessed some interesting moments with unsuspecting guests who did not know how to pace themselves to get through the marathon meal. As mean as it may sound now, we boys actually judged guests by how well they survived our "ordeal of food." A few did quite well. Many, alas, did not. The ones most prone to failure were the innocent girlfriends my cousin or my brothers would bring to a family Christmas, Thanksgiving, or Easter celebration. You would look at the skinny ones and know that they were doomed from the start.

No matter which of those holidays we were celebrating, the meal always began with soup, usually a big bowl of chicken broth with pastina and little meatballs, called wedding soup by some. After the soup came the antipasto, a large plate heavy with sliced meats—salami, mortadella, prosciutto, and capicola—and mozzarella, provolone, and Gorgonzola cheeses. This was served with pickled and fried peppers, olives, fried egg balls, and loaves of crusty bread.

We were just beginning. This was followed by a salad of mixed greens with garlic and red wine vinegar dressing. Then came the homemade pasta. It might be lasagna, sometimes made with hard-boiled eggs and sliced meatballs in place of the ricotta cheese and ground meat, or it might be a pan of crepe-like cannelloni with a cheese and spinach stuffing. Sometimes we had handmade ravioli. Of course a big bowl of meatballs and braciola would be passed around to enjoy with the pasta.

Even though our family had eaten like this for decades, Mom would warn us to pace ourselves. We were certainly quick eaters—Mom would start to mutter something about "two weeks of cooking and you're going to be done in less than an hour. Madonna di Carm!"—but we did begin to slow down. We learned to taste just a little of everything and to never, never go back for seconds. If you followed this rule, you were okay. Newcomers, unaware of the rule, usually were full and contented at the end of the pasta course, thinking—as the dinner dishes were collected and quickly washed—that dessert and coffee awaited them now that this great Italian feast was finished.

But the cleaned plates would reappear in front of us. Then, without warning, out would come the "American" part of the meal. Depending on the holiday, it could be turkey or ham or lamb or any combination of the three, with all the trimmings. Mom's turkey dressing, made with the bird's innards, breadcrumbs, cheese, and lots of eggs, was a meal in itself that usually weighed more than the turkey it stuffed. There were mashed potatoes and sweet potatoes and, for some inexplicable reason, Brussels sprouts (how they made it to our table, Mom never explained). Hot dinner rolls and stalks of fennel (called finocchio, or licorice celery) made the rounds as well.

The newcomers never could completely hide their look of disbelief and terror. Some would bravely take a little bit of the food and push it around their plates, hoping that no one would notice it wasn't making it to their lips. Others would suddenly become very interested in the conversations going on around them and would talk rather than eat. Others gamely tried to keep up, which from time to time led to disaster.

The meal would finally wind down. As if on cue, the men would go to the living room to nap, the women to the kitchen to wash all the dishes, and the children to play.

Fresh fruit and nuts would be put on the table to "tide people over" until dessert. On occasion a strange tribal rite would occur: the adult males would have a competition on the living room rug to see who could stand on his head the longest. It was a bizarre sight. My brothers and I would run to collect all the change that fell out of their pockets. If the meal didn't scare off the new guests, this competition usually did. It may also explain why generations of men in our family were not very tall.

Once the bragging rights were secured, we'd gather back at the table for ice cream cake or lemon pie or store-bought cannoli. This was our way of celebrating the holidays.

Even when times were tough, we did not pinch pennies on the holidays. In those difficult times, the table laden with savory dishes and surrounded by family and friends became the ultimate symbol of hope. Shouldn't our faith lead us to the same realization? In times of abundant blessings as well as in moments of difficulty, we come to God's table, believing that we will be sustained. Simply being there is how we live out our hope, how we demonstrate what it means for God to love us.

8

THE IMPORTANCE
OF LEFTOVERS

As I sat in the kitchen of a retired couple's simple apartment and enjoyed the flavors and freshness of a home-cooked Polish Sunday dinner, I realized that this meal was costing them more than they could afford on their fixed income. When my friend Jack and I had been invited to dinner here, I knew that this would be the case. So, in a small way, we hoped to make up for it. Between the two of us, we brought wine, a bottle of brandy, a box of candy, some mixed nuts, a fruit basket, and some fresh-cut flowers. At the end of our visit the couple offered to send us home with the leftovers. We saw the relief on their faces when we begged off, both of us claiming that we weren't going straight home and that we feared the food would spoil. In this way, we ensured that they would get at least two or three more meals out of what they had prepared for us.

My brother tells of going to dinner at a neighbor's home in a well-to-do suburb. After a round or two of drinks, eight people sat around a formally set table. Each was served a small bowl of salad with a single slice of French bread. Then the main course of chicken breasts and baked potatoes was served family style. For eight dinner guests, nine breasts and nine potatoes were set out on platters. After everyone had served themselves a breast and a potato and eaten, it was clear that no one wanted to take either the last breast or the last spud. So they sat there on the platters looking as forlorn as my brother and the other still-hungry guests. As the hostess cleared the table, she remarked how pleased she was that almost all the food had been eaten. No one said anything. Knowing my brother, I'd guess he probably stopped for a sandwich on his way home.

In our family, leftovers were an essential part of growing up. On Sunday evenings, Mom would simply reheat leftovers. Any of us who might still be hungry never minded another helping of pasta. Other times during the week she would cook enough so that there would be food for another meal. This was especially necessary before the advent of microwave ovens and the convenience foods we would prepare in them. It made sense to cook larger portions during an era in which almost everything was made from scratch.

Beyond the fact that leftovers were more practical back in those days, there was and still is another good reason to make sure there are leftovers. When we cook so abundantly, everyone is guaranteed to have their fill. When there is still food on the table after everyone is done eating, it also communicates to the guests that nothing has been held back, including love. The guests' presence is celebrated not only by the food that has been served to them, but also by the food that remains. Storage bags and plastic containers provide convenient ways to invite guests to take some of the abundance home with them. For me, leftovers are also a subtle way of finding out what my guests really liked. They politely ate what they were served and said positive things. But what they pack up to take home with them is a true indicator of the dishes they enjoyed the most.

Liturgists tell us that at Mass the celebrant should consecrate only the bread and wine needed for that celebration. Only what is needed for the sick should be placed in the tabernacle after communion. That makes sense on many levels. But I worry about running out and having to break the consecrated Hosts into small pieces to accommodate everyone coming to receive Holy Communion. When there is Eucharist in the sacred vessel after everyone has received Holy Communion, it seems to me to mirror what happened when Jesus multiplied the loaves and fish, and many baskets were left over. It is also a sign of the abundant love that God has for us and that we share. We don't need to worry that it will run out. There is always more than enough for all of us.

I know that some folks will disagree with me. In a world where people go hungry every night and many die of starvation, what right do I have to promote leftovers? In a world where resources are growing scarce, how could I appear to condone such wastefulness? Even liturgically, I can be accused of a misguided theology of the Eucharist. But I am not suggesting that people overeat or that leftovers be thrown out or wasted. Good, home-cooked meals shared with others ultimately use less of the world's resources than what we get in fast-food establishments or what we buy premade and frozen.

Leftovers, it is true, are always a little messy. But that is okay. Their flavors do fade, so they must be consumed in a timely way. It is sad to throw away what someone has given you because it sat in the back of the refrigerator—or in the back of your heart—for too long. Ultimately, the abundance that we share is not so much the food itself, but what it represents, and that is love freely and completely given, not portioned out in neat little servings. Imagine if God parceled out love to us or held some of it back for whatever reason.

So when you come to my home for dinner, come hungry and expect to take some food and love home with you. And when we worship together, may we come forward for the Eucharist confident in our faith that Jesus is here for everyone. And then let us all take that loving presence with us out of the church and share it with others, over and over again.

FIRST COURSE

Then he took the five loaves and the two fish, raised his eyes to heaven, and said the blessing over them; then he broke them and handed them to his disciples to distribute among the crowd. They all ate as much as they wanted, and when the scraps remaining were collected they filled twelve baskets.

LUKE 9:16–17

*O*ne can never thank Marco Polo enough for bringing the gift of pasta home with him after traveling to China. Inventive Italian cooks over the years have created many forms of pasta, with colorful names like radiatori (shaped like radiators), orecchiette (shaped like little ears), and farfalle (shaped like bow ties).

Pasta, part of the **first course**, is the heart of the Italian meal. Perhaps it is the carbohydrates pumping through our systems along with the sugar in the sauce, but eating pasta is soothing and fulfilling. It is hard to stay angry at a person when you are sharing a steaming bowl of pasta with them. A good Italian meal always has bowls of pasta left over on the table. The spirit of *abbondanza*—of sharing all of God's gifts and graces—is always evident.

JERRY'S "AWARD-WINNING" BREAD

My friend Jerry never cooks, not even in his microwave. But every year for the holidays he bakes this bread for his large family and his friends. It is sweet and festive and tastes great sliced, toasted, and buttered. And it proves that anyone can share their love, because anyone can find something to cook and bring to others. Wrap the loaves in colored foil and bring them as a gift, or serve them warm from the oven.

Makes about 8 loaves

INGREDIENTS

4 packages dry yeast

2 cups sugar plus 1 tablespoon sugar

1/2 cup water, lukewarm

4 cups milk, warmed

2 tablespoons salt

12 cups all-purpose flour plus 4 cups all-purpose flour

8 eggs plus 1 egg

1 teaspoon nutmeg

1 cup golden raisins, soaked in hot water

1 pound unsalted butter, melted

DIRECTIONS

In a bowl, combine the yeast, 1 tablespoon of the sugar, and the water and set aside to grow frothy.

Pour the milk into a large mixing bowl. Add the yeast mixture, the salt, and 4 cups of the flour.

Let the mixture rise for 1 hour, or until double in size.

Beat 8 of the eggs with the remaining 2 cups of sugar; add to the mixture.

Sift the remaining 12 cups of flour with the nutmeg; add to the mixture. Mix well. Add the raisins.

Add the butter and work it into the dough.

Let the dough rise for 1 hour, or until doubled.

Preheat oven to 350°F.

Separate the dough and place it into greased loaf pans. The number of pans depends on how the dough rises. Each loaf pan should be a little more than half full, so that the dough will rise to the top of the pan.

Beat the remaining egg and brush it over the tops of the loaves before baking.

Bake the loaves for about 45 minutes, or until a beautiful golden brown.

My Own (Cheating) Tomato Sauce with Neck Bones

This sauce takes care of my craving for neck bones. I served it to my brother Joe after he was discharged from the hospital; I'd like to believe it helped him heal. Good meals do that.

For cooking the sauce, you'll need a heat diffuser (sometimes called a scorch pad). This is a metal pad that is placed between the heat source, whether gas flame or electric coil, and your stockpot. Diffusers can be purchased at many kitchen stores. They prevent scorching of the pot's ingredients; once food is scorched, it is impossible to eliminate that burnt taste from whatever is in the pot.

The longer the neck bones cook, the richer the sauce will be. If you can cook this a day ahead and refrigerate it, it will taste even better reheated. Skim the excess fat before reheating.

INGREDIENTS

4 pounds pork and/or beef neck bones

Olive oil

Salt and pepper

Italian seasoning

4 or 5 (26-ounce) jars marinara sauce

2 (15-ounce) cans diced tomatoes, plain or with basil and/or garlic

1 cup dry red wine

3/4 cup grated Romano or Parmesan cheese, plus additional for topping

1 sweet onion, peeled and whole

1/2 cup sugar

Orecchiette or spaghetti

DIRECTIONS

Baste the neck bones with olive oil and season with salt, pepper, and Italian seasoning. Bake in the oven at 350°F until meat is slightly pink, 45 minutes or longer, depending on how much meat is on the bones. If the meat is baked for too short a time, it will be tough in the sauce; if baked for too long, it will dry out on the bone.

While the meat is in the oven, mix the marinara sauce and the diced tomatoes in a large stockpot. Place a heat diffuser over the burner and cook the sauce in the pot over low heat.

Add the wine, the cheese, the onion, and the sugar, stirring often.

When the neck bones are done, add them to the sauce, and cook over low heat with the pot covered until the meat is ready to fall off the bones.

Cook the pasta of your choice according to instructions.

Remove the bones from the sauce and set aside. Pour the sauce over the pasta and serve with grated cheese and the neck bones.

MOM'S PIZZA PIE

This stuffed pizza could be the most unique pizza you'll ever eat. It is a lot of work, but it's worth it! Save time by going to your neighborhood pizzeria (not a chain delivery service) or a specialty grocery store and purchasing pre-made dough. If you choose to make the dough yourself, the portion that is left over can be used to make a loaf of bread, or you can roll it out and top it with your favorite toppings for a great regular pizza.

This recipe calls for pitted Italian dry olives, which are little wrinkly black olives that can be found with other bulk olives at various specialty grocery stores. Regular pitted black olives are fine as a substitute but are not nearly as good.

INGREDIENTS

STUFFING

4 or 5 sweet onions, sliced

$1/2$ cup olive oil

1 large can whole Italian-style plum tomatoes

$1/2$ teaspoon crushed garlic

$3/4$ teaspoon dried basil

$3/4$ teaspoon parsley

$1/2$ pound pitted Italian dry olives, sliced

DOUGH

2 whole potatoes, peeled and cut into $1/2$-inch cubes

1 cup chicken broth

$2^1/2$ pounds Ceresota all-purpose unbleached flour plus
2 pounds Ceresota unbleached flour

2 packages dry yeast

$1/2$ teaspoon salt

DIRECTIONS FOR STUFFING

Place the onions in a frying pan with the olive oil; cover and cook. Do not allow the onions to brown.

Mash the tomatoes from the can and add to the onions, cooking until tender.

Add the garlic, the basil, the parsley, and the olives. Cook uncovered for 5 minutes and then set aside. To drain off excess liquid, you may place the stuffing in a sieve over a bowl.

DIRECTIONS FOR DOUGH

Add the potatoes and the chicken broth to a pot; add water to cover the potatoes. Boil the potatoes. Reserve the liquid to use when mashing potatoes and making the dough.

Place 2¹/₂ pounds of the flour in a bowl and add the yeast. Add the salt and mix the dry ingredients by hand.

Using a mixer, mash the cooked potatoes with some of the cooking liquid, then set aside to cool to room temperature.

Create a well in the dry mixture and begin to slowly add the potatoes, working them together by hand a little at a time. Continuously add the liquid to the mixture, working it into the dough a little at a time.

When the dough begins to form a ball, remove it from the bowl and knead it on a floured cutting board.

Slowly add the remaining 2 pounds of flour and the liquid to the growing dough.

Fold and punch the dough until it becomes elastic. Kneading time depends on the dough and other conditions, such as temperature and humidity. When the dough is ready, it should stretch easily without tearing.

Oil a large bowl with olive oil and place the dough in the bowl, rotating the dough in the oil until it is coated. Cover the bowl with a paper towel and let stand for 30 minutes.

DIRECTIONS FOR BAKING

Oil the sides and the bottom of a pan that is 15 inches long, 10 inches wide, and 3 inches deep—about the size of a full-sized cookie sheet.

Return the dough to the cutting board; cut the dough in thirds. Set aside one-third for making a loaf of bread or a regular pizza.

Roll out the second one-third portion of the dough to the size of the bottom of the pan plus 1 inch all around. Place the rolled dough into the oiled pan so that it extends up the sides about 1 inch. Press the dough down firmly, leaving indentations in the bottom to hold the juices of the stuffing mix.

Roll out the remaining one-third portion of the dough to the size of the top of the pan.

Using a spoon with holes so that excess liquid is left in the bowl, place the cooled stuffing mixture into the dough in the pan, covering the bottom. If the stuffing has been sitting in a sieve, do not press out the liquid before spooning the stuffing into the dough.

Place the top layer of rolled dough over the mixture, folding the lip of the bottom dough over the top dough. Pinch the dough all around to seal it tight. Puncture the top layer with a knife 6 to 8 times to let steam escape during cooking.

Cover the completed pizza with a towel and set aside to rise for another hour or more (depending on the weather and the temperature and humidity in the house), or place the pizza in a warm oven to rise.

When the pizza has risen to double in size and the dough bounces back to the touch, place it in the oven at 350°F and cook until the crust is golden brown.

Cool slightly before cutting into squares.

9

SPIRIT WEEK

I enjoyed my thirteen years of teaching in the high
school seminary. I was young and energetic. During
those years I learned more than I taught, from both the
students and the faculty. But I still look back with shock
at some of the things we did.

In the dead of winter, after the holidays and before
the spring thaw, when everyone felt oppressed by the gray
skies and snow, the administration would hold what was
known as Mini-Course Week. Students would sign up
for a number of unique classes, the topics of which were
limited only by the creativity, talent, and resourceful-
ness of the faculty. There were courses in origami, CPR,
changing your car's oil, directing a play, and much more.
I taught creative writing and meditation and led a tour of
Chicago.

One of the priests taught a class in bachelor survival—
the course that brought a permanent end to Mini-Course

Week. While making coffee he somehow started a fire that caused no serious damage but set off the alarms and emptied the school. We stood out in the cold as fire trucks arrived from all over the city. An hour later, we were allowed to return to the building. The following year, there was no Mini-Course Week.

Still, we needed a midwinter break from the dreariness and the routine. So Mini-Course Week was replaced by Spirit Week, which the student government organized and ran. It consisted of pep rallies and many lunch-period and after-school activities. I found myself off in a corner supervising the tricycle races, which attracted mostly freshmen. The reason I'd been relegated to the fringes of the action was that I had objected to some of the food-related contests that I thought were offensive and a little too dangerous. After all, we Italians take our eating seriously. It is not the stuff of games. I was overruled and accused of lacking spirit.

So when the tricycle races rolled to a halt, I ambled over to the cafeteria to see how bad the contests in question really were. One of the safer of the events—a contest to determine who could eat the most ice cream bars in a minute—was won by Fr. Mike, who beat all of his student challengers, thanks to a one-minute tiebreaker. In all, he ate more than seven frozen bars. Later that afternoon, as he was coaching the wrestling team, his teeth started hurting. I wonder why.

That contest was followed by one involving Jell-O. Each contestant had to eat a large bowl of cherry Jell-O while lying facedown on the floor with his hands behind his back, then get up and run to the timekeeper and shout, "There's always room for Jell-O!" This contest was all the more challenging because the Jell-O had been made with garlic salt instead of sugar.

Then came the hot-pepper-eating contest. Contestants had to eat six peppers, each one hotter than the last. One student ran outside after eating a "level four" pepper and threw his face into a pile of drifted snow. Only Fr. John—who summered in Mexico and had brought the peppers for the contest—made it through the sixth level.

There was one competition left. At first glance it appeared pretty tame, but it may have been the most dangerous of all. It was the prune-eating contest. This seemed just plain cruel, because the competition would be over long before the ultimate outcome. Participants were lined up at tables across from their judge. The first contestant to unscrew a jar of prunes, eat them all, drink the remaining prune juice, and turn over the empty jar would be the winner. I refused to be a judge. I just stood there watching until I realized that the prunes were not pitted, and one student was swallowing the pits as he ate the prunes. I told the judge to make him stop. Then I told the student to stop. But all the cheering and laughing kept him going. He had the fastest time but was disqualified because of me. He said he felt fine. His supporters thought I was a stick-in-the-mud.

That evening I called his home and told his mother to watch him. I told her what he had done. To my surprise, she laughed and asked why I was so worried. The next day our deposed prune-eating champion did show up for school. I asked him how his night had been. He offered me a weak smile and told me in a soft voice that at about three in the morning he thought he had, as he so graphically put it, "cracked the porcelain." With that, he excused himself and headed toward the bathroom. By the end of the school day he seemed to be back to his regular self—no pun intended—with no permanent harm done.

The next year I became part of the administrative team, and I found myself on the scheduling committee. Resurrecting Mini-Course Week was still out of the question, and I was convinced that Spirit Week carried even more dangers. So we put together a nice four-day Midwinter Madness weekend off, with school closed Friday through Monday. The thinking was that it was much safer for us to get away from one another. At least, that is how I saw it from a lounge chair in sunny Florida during that midwinter break.

I do remember some activities at Spirit Week that worked, such as the toy drive and the food drive, both of which tapped the students' inherent idealism. Wrapping toys or carrying cases of food in a procession to be blessed and sent on their way allowed the students to experience making a difference in the lives of people outside their limited circle.

But I couldn't see how spirit could grow in cruel and bizarre competition. The Spirit we long for and seek grows through mutual respect, care, and concern—qualities that were sorely lacking at Spirit Week, as people tried to eat too many hot chilies or whole jars of prunes. But maybe what really bothered me was seeing people eat food and not enjoy it at all.

To Feed
the Hungry

*B*ack when I taught at the high school seminary, the faculty would take students to the Uptown neighborhood in Chicago to help out with the Catholic Workers during Lent. For decades, Uptown was a point of entry, home to some of the poorest people in the city. St. Thomas of Canterbury Parish reflected the amazing diversity of the area, and the Catholic Workers were there to be of assistance and to live out the gospel message by working, living, and eating with the poor, as Dorothy Day and Peter Maurin had taught them. In addition to the poor and the homeless who populated the neighborhood, there were growing numbers of the mentally ill who had been released from area hospitals and institutions after the state stopped funding their care. They moved to the cheap hotels and rooming houses that were spread throughout the neighborhood. Some just lived on the streets.

The Catholic Workers offered what they called a parish family meal every Wednesday evening. They did not want this to appear in any way as a demeaning soup line, so those coming to eat were seated at tables, and volunteers brought them food and beverages. The Catholic Workers served whatever had been donated, no matter how much or how little, knowing that all of it would be eaten and believing that the Holy Spirit would provide enough food for them to host another meal the next week.

The faculty and the seminary students from our school would meet with the Catholic Workers prior to the meal. They would serve us first and then assign us jobs as dishwashers, waiters, or busboys. This experience was always an eye-opener for our students. One night, when I was helping as a waiter, it became an education for me.

Among the three hundred or so folks being served that night were a young mother and her two beautiful children. Clearly they were homeless—their clothes were tattered and threadbare—but she could not share any of that with me, for fear that the Department of Children and Family Services would be called in and her children would be taken away from her. So I didn't ask.

I brought them food. This happened to be a good night: there was a stew with a lot of meat and vegetables, as well as pasta, day-old bakery bread, salad, and apples (for those with teeth good enough to eat them). No one would go away hungry.

The mother gently made sure that I served her children first. Their smiles were brief and perfunctory; what they wanted to do was eat. Incredibly, they waited until I brought their mother her plate, and then they started to eat quickly. I grew busy serving others.

When I looked back at them a few moments later, all their food was gone. So I went over to the mother and told her not to worry: everyone had been served, and there were plenty of leftovers. To my utter astonishment she politely but firmly thanked me and told me that it wouldn't be necessary to bring them more food. The children heard her, and their anticipation quickly turned to disappointment. But neither of them said a word. I thought that she had misunderstood me, so again I told her that the food was there for them and that I would be happy to bring more. Everyone around them was being served seconds by now, and some were putting extra apples in their pockets to eat later.

My exasperation mingled with anger when she refused my offer a second time. I began to wonder what kind of mother she was, denying her children—who clearly were still hungry—a nourishing meal. Was it a control issue? Was she just being mean? No matter what her reason might be, I felt that her action bordered on child abuse. So I grew louder and angrier.

She stood up then and walked me out of earshot of the children. With no little sadness in her voice, she asked me if I had ever had to deal with little children going to sleep hungry, begging for food and then crying and whimpering until they fell asleep, exhausted. I told her that tonight her children could sleep well with full stomachs. Didn't she want that?

With a deep sigh she just shook her head. "You just don't get it, do you? I can't allow my children the luxury of going to bed satisfied. I can't let them get used to it, because more than likely tomorrow night, and the next night, and the next, they won't get a meal like tonight. They may not get anything at all. And they will be miserable. I have to keep them used to being hungry. I have to be tough." As tough as she was, one little tear formed in the corner of her eye.

What could I say in response? I cannot remember ever going to bed hungry, unless I was going through one of my many unsuccessful attempts at dieting. I watched her help her children put on their coats. I saw the uncomplaining looks of disappointment on their faces. I watched them walk out the door.

I looked for them when I brought another group of students the following month, but they weren't there. In fact, I never saw them again. Had their luck changed and they no longer needed the meal? I doubt it. Maybe they just moved on in an effort to escape Chicago's streets and harsh winters. Maybe someone did call the state and the children were taken away from their mother. More than likely I had scared her away from one guaranteed decent meal per week.

When the volunteers sat around after the cleanup to discuss the evening, one of the Catholic Workers asked the students what they had learned that night. Everyone gave me puzzled looks when I offered that good intentions are often not enough. Those two children had gone home hungry that night, and my gut told me I should have done something more for them.

When we are brought face-to-face with the hunger and the hopelessness that are a result of evil, we have to use what God has given us to make a difference. And that is not always easy to do.

I have never experienced personally what that mother and her children were living. Yes, there is power in a good meal lovingly prepared and served. But sometimes we must face the fact that more needs to be done and that we must find a way to do it. These solutions go beyond the feel-good experience of occasionally working at a soup kitchen. From there we must go to the causes of injustice and eradicate them.

11

TABLE MANNERS

*O*ne year the priests in my rectory hosted a woman whose writing, teaching, and powerful speaking had gained her a reputation as a prophet who worked for justice. For many good workers in the vineyard, she was a living saint. One of the priests with whom I was living and working had attended a class she had taught in Louisiana. Now she was coming to Chicago for a conference, and she was going to stay in a guest room in our rectory to save the expense of a hotel room.

The woman had some health concerns, so we prepared her meals from a list she gave us of the foods she could eat. For breakfast she wanted only fruit. I went to the store before she arrived and brought home bananas, oranges, and pears, which I would combine with the apples that a family in the parish had given us from a relative's farm.

The next morning, before I had even met her, I laid out a nice spread of freshly washed fruit. Some of the apples were bruised, so I set them aside to later peel, sprinkle with lemon juice, cinnamon, and Grape-Nuts, and then bake in the oven for a nice snack. A fresh pot of herbal tea was brewing when she came into the kitchen. Fr. Mike introduced her to me. I was struck by the confident way in which she carried herself, but it was her voice that really got to me. Every word rang clear, like a brass bell on a cold morning. Her speaking was so precise that I felt as if I were hearing every letter of every word she spoke. I was certain she could read the phone book and make it sound like Shakespeare.

After looking around the kitchen—more like surveying it—she reached into the garbage and pulled out some of the apples I had thought were too far gone to serve her or to use in my snack. Then she started lecturing me about being wasteful. She grabbed a knife and proceeded to show me how much good fruit remained on those apples I had thrown away. I felt duly chastised by her words and by the look of embarrassment Fr. Mike was throwing my way. But when she asked me if my mother hadn't taught me any better, I kind of snapped.

I thought of Mom bringing home from the family store all the broken eggs, the meat too brown to sell, the dented cans of soup, the bruised and soft fruit and wilted vegetables. It was the food no one else would buy, and yet she turned it into delicious meals. I remembered how she would reverently kiss any bread she had to throw out because it had gotten moldy or had fallen onto the floor. All bread was sacred to her because the priest consecrated bread into the body of Christ. I pictured the time I visited my mom and found a box of candy bars in the refrigerator. When I asked her about them, she told me softly that as a child doing piecework in the Endicott-Johnson shoe factory she was too poor to buy a candy bar during their break. Now that she could afford them, she wanted to have a box of them on hand for her grandchildren.

But most of all I remembered Mom teaching us by example that when family or friends or any guests came to your home, they were always to be served the best and as much of it as they desired, even if that meant there would be a little less for you. And you were never to make anyone feel uncomfortable, no matter what you felt or thought.

At this point in my encounter with the saintly woman, that last part of Mom's lesson was lost on me. As the woman finished lecturing me, I took the kettle from the stove and poured us both a cup of tea, which wasn't steaming nearly as much as I was. For some reason I felt the need to defend both my mother and myself. I forced a smile that I hoped would indicate that I not only had heard her but was also properly contrite. She smiled back at me, but I thought I detected some condescension in it.

Then I said, "Let me tell you about my mother. Not only would she have never thought of serving you fruit that was bruised or anything that was less than the very best—because you always treat guests as special, and the food that you serve is a sign of how much you love and respect them—but if she were in your shoes she would also have eaten what was put in front of her, enjoyed it, and thanked her host profusely for that hospitality. That's what my mother would have done. Now, please excuse me, and do enjoy your breakfast with Fr. Mike." I glanced over at Fr. Mike, who for once in his life looked as if he had no appetite at all.

Mom would not have been proud of me. I violated the cardinal rule of always making guests feel comfortable. I should have waited until after she had left to vent to Fr. Mike or someone else, or saved it for a story I would write years later.

No one has the corner on wisdom or sanctity, and I guess even a saint can have a bad morning—which she did, in my mind. And if a saint can stumble like that, then what do you expect of me, someone to whom the word *saintly* has never been applied? I know that is not much of a defense, but it's the best I have, that and the truism that you can never criticize an Italian man's mother to his face. In any case, the woman left for her conference after breakfast, so I didn't see her again. Fr. Mike knew better than to say anything to me about it. And those apples I baked in the oven? They tasted very sweet that night, very sweet indeed.

12

AN UNFORGETTABLE MEAL

What do you do with fifty high school seminary students who want to be of service to others in any way they can? After an especially effective senior class retreat, our students were looking for a way to channel their idealism and energy as they continued to focus on what God was calling them to do with their lives. I am not sure how it was decided, but they selected a parish at which to have a special liturgy for anointing the sick, followed by a festive meal for all in attendance. This meal would be set up, cooked, served, and cleaned up by the students. But what was supposed to be a simple meal of hearty soup, fresh-baked bread, and cookies baked by the mothers of the students grew into a more complex menu. The soup became an elaborate stew-like concoction, which one of the students claimed was an old family recipe. A team of students did the shopping and the preparation and cooked the stew in the institutional-sized pots in the church social hall.

I watched with interest and growing alarm as the students threw whole tomatoes, dozens of beets, and stalks of celery into a pot already filled with frozen fish fillets, chicken stock, cream, and much more. The student overseeing the process seemed sure of himself, but I had my doubts.

It was turning out to be a crazy day. The weather would not cooperate, so many of those who were coming to be blessed needed to be picked up and brought to the church. One of our students arrived late, walking his bicycle and carrying about ten loaves of banged-up French bread. He had hit a car while trying to ride his bike and carry the bread at the same time. He insisted that he was unhurt, but his bicycle was pretty battered. No one knew how to turn on the sound system in the church, which was essential if the many elderly in attendance were to hear and take part in the liturgy. With these other concerns to deal with, I left the cooks to their own devices.

The Mass itself went well. The students were touchingly gentle as they helped those who needed aid come forward and receive the sacrament of anointing. The students proclaimed the readings, led the singing, reflected on the Gospel, and threw themselves into the entire service with the enthusiasm and the idealism that are graces of the young.

When they brought everyone to the hall for the meal, the food smelled delicious. My only concern was that the crowd was almost double what we had prepared for. So I invoked the old FHB rule—"Family Holds Back." The students were not to eat until all of the guests had been served. I assured the always-hungry students that if there were not enough leftovers, I would order pizzas for them after the guests had left.

As it turned out, every bit of the stew was served, every crust of bread was eaten, and every cookie was devoured or carried home in purses or pockets, leaving fifty hungry but satisfied students feeling that they had done something good. After cleaning up and getting all the people home, we gathered for a self-congratulatory meal of pizza and soda. The following Monday we would meet after school and evaluate what had happened, determine what we had learned from it, and decide what the next project would be.

The calls started coming in on Sunday morning and continued through the day and into Monday. By meeting time we had learned that more than forty of the people who had been anointed and stayed for dinner needed anointing again: they had food poisoning. Five of them had had to be hospitalized. It became clear then what our next project had to be: hospital visits and get-well notes.

The students who had been in charge of the cooking were devastated, having been demoted from honored cooks to food poisoners. It was quite a fall from grace. The poor guy who had brought the recipe muttered something about how he had been unsure if the recipe called for five pounds of fresh *beets* or five pounds of fresh *beef*. I told him that even if he had been mistaken, all the beets would not have been responsible for the sickness. It was more likely a problem with the fish.

The students expected the worst when they went to make all those visits to the sick, but they returned from the homes and the hospital with the good news that most of the afflicted were taking it in stride and even found it humorous that the students, because they had so generously refrained from eating, hadn't gotten sick at all. These young seminarians had received a crash course in tolerance, forgiveness, and the wisdom of the elderly.

Everyone learned a great deal that week. I don't think any students in that group ended up in the priesthood, but I'll bet that most of them still remember trying to help people and getting them sick instead. Most of all, I hope they remember that they served a memorable meal, in more ways than one.

Sometimes the best meals are those that do not turn out as planned. If we fight it when things go awry, the meal has the potential to become a major disaster. If we are a little bit lucky and can adapt and be flexible, we might be able to save the situation. The same is true at important times in our lives. When things appear to be turning out not as we had hoped, we need to step back and find God's grace in it all.

13

THE TRUTH ABOUT
EGGPLANT

*L*et me begin by mixing fruits and vegetables and saying that the proverb "The apple doesn't fall far from the tree" fits this tale about the abuse of the word *eggplant*, or *melanjon* in Italian. Sometimes people ask me where I got the trait of being so outspoken. I tell them they should have met my mother. This story relates how her outspokenness landed her in the newspaper.

One summer about twenty-five years ago, some friends took my parents to the city-sponsored Festa Italiana at the lakefront in Chicago, where you could eat a sausage sandwich with roasted peppers, ride a Ferris wheel, buy a baby bib that read "I love pasta," and listen to Julius la Rosa sing "Eh, Cumpari!" live, just as he did more than fifty years ago—all in one place.

Mom was walking along, having a good time, when she saw a crowd gathering and cheering. She stepped around those who were taller than she was, or everyone over the age of eight, to see what was going on. It was an old-fashioned dunk tank. The crowd had gathered to cheer on the contestants, who had bought three balls for a dollar in hopes of hitting the bull's-eye and dropping the jeering person in the tank into the water. My mother had never liked the concept, something I would learn decades later when I sat in a similar tank as a pastor to raise money for my then-struggling parish. But someone had attached a sign to this dunk tank at the Festa Italiana, and that sign angered Mom more than the dunking did.

The small hand-lettered sign read DUNK THE MELANJON! It's important to point out that the people sitting in the dunk tank were black, and mainly white folks were throwing the balls. This was bad enough. But the sign was referring to the man in the tank as *melanjon*, the Italian word for eggplant and a pejorative that some Italians use to label a person of color.

Mom pushed her way up to the front and, placing her hands on her hips, told all who were in hearing range how inappropriate the sign was and how low-class it made them look and how embarrassed she was at that moment to be Italian. Then, with a look that dared anyone to come near her, she stepped over to the tank, ripped the sign down, and started to walk away. She was small but brave.

As it happened, a reporter from one of Chicago's daily newspapers was within earshot. He came up to her as she walked away from the scene and asked her what the fuss was about. She told him about the sign and showed the pieces of it to him. He asked her if it was a racial epithet. She replied simply with "What do you think?" and walked away. She didn't know that the reporter had been drawn to the crowd and the excitement before she had arrived. When he saw the sign he had asked for a translation from a number of people who had gathered around the tank, but no one would tell him what it meant. The reporter never got Mom's name. His article in the paper the next day described the righteous anger of a white-haired little Italian lady who challenged the racism, both overt and unconscious, of her country folk at their annual festival. She alone stood up to it, challenged it, and demanded that it stop. She was embarrassed by the article but relieved that it didn't reveal her name. It pleased her, though, to read that the sign had not been replaced. She refused to go to another Festa after that.

Fast-forward a few decades. By now a priest, I received a phone call from a representative of the Italian American organization that cosponsored the Festa. He asked me if I would like to concelebrate the Mass that would take place before the event. I remembered my mom and her adamant refusal to attend ever again. I asked with as innocent a voice as I could muster if there was going to be a dunk tank this year. Yes, there would be. I told him the story of the sign, and he assured me that such a sign would not be appearing this year. But that wasn't enough for me. I told the rep that unless the only people in the tank were the queen of the Festa and her court, an Italian monsignor, and assorted others whose names ended in a vowel, I would not consider concelebrating the Eucharist, much less attending the Festa. He hung up on me. Not only have I never been invited to another Festa, but I also stopped receiving an invitation to the Columbus Day parade as well. I guess my remarks traveled.

That's all right. Now I go to the Italian street festivals in the old neighborhoods where Louis Prima's daughter is advertised as the headliner. I enjoy the rice balls and the stuffed mushrooms and—occasionally, when it's on the menu—the roasted eggplant. That is the sign I like to see. And, thank God, there isn't a dunk tank in sight.

I remember hearing kids on the playground taunt me when I was young with "Hey, greaseball, why did you drop the ball? Still got tomato sauce on your hands?" and "Your momma rolls meatballs for the Mafia." I remember being hurt and angry. I remember going home in tears and Mom telling me that they were just jealous because they were eating bologna sandwiches. It made me feel better. She taught me to be proud of who I was and that putting down other people just made you low-class. I know that we all have prejudices. We need to own them and then act to rid ourselves of them. Even when we stumble over them, we can never surrender to them.

14

ADAPTATIONS

I've seen it before and I'll probably see it again, as the students I taught in high school years ago rush headlong into their forties—people leaving behind their family traditions and cultures and adapting to a more generic American way of life. Among the former students I've seen change in this way, Andy stands out. He was an honor student, a superior soccer player, and a class leader. I taught him religion, coached him in soccer, and helped him with his delivery of an outstanding valedictorian speech at graduation. After high school, he studied law. His parents, who had been born in eastern Europe, had high expectations of Andy from the beginning, but for whatever reason, they provided him with little ongoing affirmation. He always got support from a priest he had stayed in close contact with from high school, but when that priest died, much of the support in Andy's life died too.

A few years ago, I heard from another former student that Andy's dad had died and was being waked, even as his mother lay in the hospital in critical condition. So I drove to the small ethnic funeral home to pay my respects, not only in my name but also in the name of the priest who couldn't be there to console Andy. Sometimes the Holy Spirit points you in the right direction, and even more rarely, you listen and follow through. The moment I arrived at the wake, I knew it was where I belonged that day.

Andy was both delighted and surprised to see me. When I told him I was there not just for me but also for his deceased friend and mentor, he cried. I looked at the collage of pictures of his father and family; there on the bottom was a small picture of the priest, Fr. Jack.

A short time later, I found myself back at that funeral home, for the wake of Andy's mother. This time, Andy and I agreed to stay in touch.

It is interesting to step into somebody's life that you knew back when it was mostly potential and experience how that potential has evolved. Andy is now a partner in a downtown law firm. He recently purchased a yet-to-be-built condominium in the "hot" South Loop neighborhood of Chicago. He drives a BMW and spends most of every summer on his boat, which is docked in Burnham

Harbor. He still plays soccer with his friends, who are, one by one, finding the woman of their dreams, marrying, and becoming, in Andy's words, "boring." He goes out with beautiful young women, some of them lawyers like him, who would love to develop a lasting relationship with him. But for many reasons, including having been burned once too often, he just is not ready for that. So they simply go out for sushi and red wine.

This description may make it sound as if Andy is a yuppie and nothing more, but he is also loyal, sensitive, and honest, and he retains something of his roots that sets him apart. I guess that is why I find myself joining him and his friends for something I never thought I would eat—uncooked fish.

I know it must be hard to imagine a pasta-loving person like me eating raw eel rolled in black rice and stuffed with raw lobster meat. But I do it. In fact, I'll try anything that is set before me, though Andy assures me that he orders the more moderate choices for me. I ask him not to tell me what I'm eating until after I've eaten it, and I am often grateful that I didn't know. My one concession to my Italian background is that I insist on eating these rolled-up creations with a fork and not chopsticks. After all, it was an Italian who invented the fork.

It is interesting that this guy who was raised on smoked sausage, pork, pierogi, and other not-so-healthy delights is now a champion of raw fish. Like many of us, he has left a lot of his past behind him. Why not? There's nothing left there for him to return to. Or is there?

Recently, Andy told me about a wake he attended of a friend's father. Not knowing what else to do, he stopped by a little bakery and bought a platter of kolacky for the family. He still had ingrained in him that simple notion that food can and does promote comfort and healing.

It would be too dramatic to say that there is a battle going on inside for Andy's soul—the old-world values versus the enticements of money, power, and status. Instead, Andy appears to have adapted to the world around him. I don't see anything wrong with his creature comforts and status symbols. I sense that he is not very attached to them. I see instead the same guy who values friendship and the loyalty it demands. I've personally experienced his generosity, and so has my parish. I've watched him struggle with loss on a number of levels but always with the same determination not to give up or back down. His is an old soul caught up with a boyish spirit.

I bet these qualities of Andy's that I've just described are not unlike those that allowed his father to leave the world he knew and come to a strange country to make his dreams come true. Andy's journey is more of an inner search for who he is and what to call home. I'm convinced he will find it. There is still much good and potential in him. It is my privilege to be there for him in Fr. Jack's name. But Lord, save me from eating uncooked creatures from the sea.

SECOND PLATE

Now as they were eating, Jesus took some bread, and when he had said the blessing he broke it and gave it to the disciples. "Take it and eat"; he said, "this is my body."

MATTHEW 26:26

*I*n Italy, the **second plate** is served after the antipasto and the pasta. This course consists of vegetables and meat or fish, or a combination of the two. It is somewhat comparable to the American main course, and here in the United States it is served either formally or family style. In the old days in Italy, often this food was cooked in the communal ovens in the center of the town, because the kitchens in the homes were just too small to handle all the food.

Every course in an Italian meal holds its own. The second plate is a sign of the host's good fortune and subsequent generosity. It is considered special because of the ingredients involved—meats and vegetables bought just for company. The hosts hope that this food will help create an occasion their guests will long remember.

MY OWN
ITALIAN STUFFED
PORK CHOPS

Once again, I cheat and doctor convenience foods to
save time. The goal is to serve a good meal and also have
time to sit and enjoy the company of those sharing it. If
I get stuck in the kitchen, it defeats the purpose of our
gathering around the table. Besides, I know my limitations. Cooking everything from scratch can be a daunt-
ing task.

Notice that I use as many packaged items as I can:
lemon juice, chicken broth, minced garlic, and stuffing. It
still tastes great. You don't have to be a snob about it, but
if you want to make it classy, toast some walnuts or pine
nuts and add them to the dressing.

INGREDIENTS

1 box Stove Top Stuffing

1 (14.5-ounce) can chicken broth

1 teaspoon Italian seasoning

1 teaspoon minced garlic in olive oil, plus additional for
topping

6 thick-cut pork chops, bone in

Olive oil

Salt and pepper

Bottled lemon juice

DIRECTIONS

Cook the stuffing as directed, substituting the chicken broth for water. Add the Italian seasoning and the garlic.

Butterfly-cut the pork chops by placing them flat on a cutting board and slicing each one open horizontally, creating a flap. Put the stuffing on the bottom piece, and set the top piece over the stuffing. Fill each pork chop with stuffing until some falls out as you lightly press the top layer of meat down on it.

Place the pork chops in a baking dish. Rub each chop with olive oil and season with salt and pepper (note that the stuffing already has a lot of salt in it). Sprinkle finely diced garlic over the top.

Bake the pork chops at 375°F until cooked thoroughly.

Squeeze lemon juice over the chops before serving.

My Own Garlic Roasted Potatoes

Side dishes can enhance a meal, fill a plate, and add to the feast and the fun. Pasta and risotto are not the only starches in the Italian's kitchen; we do a great job with potatoes too. I remember the potatoes that grew on my uncle's farm in southern Italy and how good they tasted.

This side dish goes well with My Own Veal Marsala (page 107), or with any meat or fish dish. When everyone eats garlic, no one has to worry. That's the real definition of community!

Ingredients

2 to 3 pounds small new potatoes

1 stick salted butter or margarine

1/3 cup olive oil

2 tablespoons minced garlic in olive oil, plus additional for topping

Salt and pepper

Chopped fresh Italian parsley, for garnish

DIRECTIONS

Boil the potatoes in salted water until they start to soften.

In a large skillet, heat the butter and the olive oil. Add the garlic.

Add the potatoes to the skillet and cook until the skins blister and the potatoes are soft, adding more butter or oil if necessary.

Season with salt and pepper and garnish with parsley. Sprinkle additional garlic over the potatoes before serving.

LOLA'S
CHICKEN VESUVIO

Lola is the wife of Nick, my brother Tony's lifelong friend. This recipe, shared at Lola and Nick's table, made it to my brother's table, where I have been able to enjoy it. It is always that way with food, stories, memories, and love: once we share them, they keep going and going and going, from one kitchen to another, from one heart to another.

This recipe calls for boneless chicken breasts. I happen to like chicken with bones, which would add cooking time both in the skillet and in the oven. Plus I would use minced garlic, lots of it, rather than powder, and I would add a little butter to the dish before baking it. Make this recipe your own, so that you can share what is uniquely yours with others.

INGREDIENTS

1 cup breadcrumbs

1 cup cornflakes

Salt and pepper

Oregano

Garlic powder

6 eggs

6 boneless, skinless chicken breasts, pounded until thin

Olive oil

3/4 cup white wine

Juice of 3 lemons

1 (14.5-ounce) can chicken broth

2 tablespoons capers

Grated Parmesan cheese

4 large Idaho potatoes, cut lengthwise into quarters

DIRECTIONS

Mix the breadcrumbs and the cornflakes in a bowl; season with salt, pepper, oregano, and garlic powder. Beat the eggs in a separate large bowl. Dip the chicken breasts into the egg and then coat the chicken with the breadcrumb mixture.

Pour enough olive oil in a frying pan to halfway cover the chicken breasts. Heat the oil over a high flame and quickly fry the chicken breasts.

Remove the chicken and carefully add the wine, the lemon juice, the chicken broth, and the capers to the pan, and season the sauce with salt, pepper, oregano, garlic powder, and Parmesan cheese. Bring to a boil.

Place the potatoes into the sauce and boil until nearly cooked.

Lay the chicken breasts and the potatoes in a casserole dish and pour the sauce from the pan over them.

Cover the casserole dish with aluminum foil and bake at 350°F for 20 minutes.

My Own
Veal Marsala

This was fun to create, and it worked the very first time I tried it. I served it to six parishioners who won my cooking them a dinner at the parish silent auction. It makes a great second plate and is easier than it looks. I remember that night and all the warm stories that followed. I hope you will have the same results.

This dish can be served with My Own Garlic Roasted Potatoes (page 102). Place the veal in the center of a platter with the potatoes around it, and pour the gravy over both. This dish will look as good as it tastes. Good presentation means you've taken the time to really care. That speaks volumes to your guests.

INGREDIENTS

Olive oil

6 eggs

1 cup all-purpose flour

Salt

1 cup Italian breadcrumbs

12 very thin veal cutlets

1 sweet onion, diced

2 tablespoons capers

2 cloves garlic, diced

1 container whole grape or cherry tomatoes

$^1/_2$ cup Marsala wine or any sweet white wine

Juice of 3 lemons

Fresh parsley, for garnish

DIRECTIONS

Beat the eggs in a large bowl. In a separate bowl, add the flour and the salt. In a third bowl, add the breadcrumbs. Set the flour aside.

Lightly coat a nonstick skillet with olive oil and place over high heat.

Dredge the cutlets through the egg, then the lightly salted flour, then the breadcrumbs.

Place the cutlets in the hot skillet and immediately add the onion, the capers, and the garlic.

Turn the cutlets over. Add the tomatoes and the wine. Decrease the heat and cook until the veal is no longer pink. Then remove the cutlets from the skillet. Overcooking will make the veal tough.

Spoon out the onion, the capers, and the tomatoes and set aside.

Add the flour left over from the dredging to the skillet with the drippings and the wine. Add the lemon juice and stir while heating to make a gravy.

Add the onion, the capers, and the tomatoes and mix. Pour the mixture over the cutlets. Garnish the dish with parsley.

Mom's Fava Beans

Here's a real peasant dish that you won't find on many menus. You'll have to soak the dried fava beans overnight, so keep that in mind if you're planning to serve this dish for a special occasion. If it's spring, use those fresh dandelion shoots I write about in chapter 3 instead of the endive.

Serve the beans directly from the pot with a wooden spoon for authenticity, and accompany the dish with a glass of robust red wine. This can be a first course or a side dish or a whole meal in itself. I think it is best eaten in the kitchen and not in a formal dining situation. You won't get more authentic than this. The dish will stick to your bones and in your memories.

Ingredients

1 pound dried fava beans, soaked overnight (*canned beans will not work*)

1 large red potato, peeled and cut into 1-inch cubes

2 cloves garlic or $1/2$ teaspoon minced garlic

2 small cans chicken broth

2 large heads endive, stemmed and cut into 2-inch pieces

1 cup olive oil

Pinch of baking soda

Loaf day-old Italian bread, cut into 1-inch cubes

DIRECTIONS

Cut the hooks off the beans and clean off any remaining skin.

Combine the potato and the beans. Rinse the mixture 3 or 4 times, until the water runs clear.

Place the potato and the beans in a stockpot. Add the garlic and the chicken broth, then add water until the beans and the potato are covered by an inch of liquid.

Cover the pot and cook over low heat for at least 3 hours. After each hour, skim off the white foam, stir 2 or 3 times, and rotate the pot over the flame to prevent scorching.

Remove the beans from the heat and stir in the olive oil and the baking soda.

Place the endive in a pot of water and boil over medium heat until tender; drain.

Blend the bean mixture with an electric blender until it is the consistency of mashed potatoes (add breadcrumbs if the mixture needs to be thickened). Stir in the endive.

Place the bean-and-endive mixture over low heat and simmer for 30 minutes.

Stir the bread into the mixture and return to low heat. Stir constantly for 15 minutes. Serve directly from the pot.

15

GRACED BY GUMBO

*W*hen I was first ordained a deacon, the seminary allowed us to suggest the style of parish at which we wanted to be assigned for our pre-priesthood internship. We could select city or suburb, the ethnic breakdown we preferred, and even the general location we desired within the archdiocese. Wanting to go back to my roots, I requested a blue-collar, North Side, lakefront parish—a parish like the one in which I had grown up. Imagine my surprise when I ended up on the Southwest Side in an African American parish.

I loved it there. The people I met were so warm and friendly and open. They had a zest for life, laughed a lot, worked hard, loved their families, and enjoyed good meals. All of this was part of my background as well. And so the following year, when it came time for me to make a similar request regarding my first assignment as an associate pastor, I hoped to be sent to another African American parish, anywhere in the city. This time I got my wish and was sent to a parish that was further south and east than the parish of my diaconate assignment. The people at my new parish were welcoming, faith filled, and eager to get involved. They were exactly what I needed as I started my ministry.

In those days it was not unusual for a rectory to employ a full-time, live-in cook and housekeeper. Ours had been formally trained as a young girl straight from Ireland. Now she was over eighty, but even at this point in her life her skills remained remarkable, despite her love of vodka. The pastor was a finicky eater, to put it mildly. His taste in food ran from the picky (no stews, no casseroles, no leftovers) to the bizarre. He insisted that the hot dogs served for lunch be peeled before they were brought to the table, because, as he said, "you never know what those meatpackers use for the skins." Believe me when I tell you that a platter of peeled, limp hot dogs looks much less appetizing than a platter of their unpeeled, plump counterparts.

My need to escape the pastor's weird tastes and partake in more normal fare would regularly lead me to the parish convent school next door, where the sisters generously allowed me to use my novice culinary talents to prepare us meals such as pasta or honey-baked chicken. The sisters' only complaint was that I was sloppy and wreaked havoc on their usually spotless kitchen. So one of them, Sr. Clare, was always assigned to stand next to me and clean up as I cooked, which I didn't mind at all.

While I was a much more adventuresome eater than the pastor, some foods were still too exotic even for me. One fateful Sunday after Mass, a family invited me to their home for dinner. He was a Chicago police officer and not a Catholic. She was originally from a long line of New Orleans Catholics. When she invited me to dinner, she asked me, hopefully, if I liked seafood gumbo. I assured her that I did, wanting to be polite, though I had never eaten gumbo in my life. Excitedly, she started to tell me all the ingredients that made her gumbo so special. I was overwhelmed. There was very little in the way of food that I did not enjoy, but her combination of fish, shrimp, crabmeat, hot links, chicken wings, ham, and okra, all cooked in a roux (whatever that was), seemed completely foreign to me.

I arrived at their house with a bottle of red wine and a bottle of white as a gift. I brought both because I wasn't sure which went with gumbo. But they were never opened. Ale, ice-cold ale, was the beverage of choice to cool down the spiciness of the gumbo and the mandatory hot sauce that accompanied it. I still remember what the aromas coming from the kitchen did to me. The odor of baking corn bread, with its nutty sweetness, seemed to wrap itself around me. But it was the earthy scent of the rich mixture of ingredients boiling in the pots of gumbo that grabbed me.

After some small talk, we sat down to eat. And I could not believe what I tasted. I knew from the start that I was eating too quickly, but I couldn't help myself. Still, the meal took up much of the evening, because I kept going back for more. Somehow, between bowls of gumbo, steaming rice, and hot sauce, the husband and I got to know one another.

I found him to be a personable guy with significant things to say. Soon we were getting together regularly to talk about the church and other things faith-related. One day he told me that he had decided to become a Catholic. We started meeting for private instruction whenever his busy schedule as a police officer allowed it. He was inquisitive, street savvy, and honest. And he eagerly embraced what he was learning.

So I was surprised and disappointed when he told me, on a rainy Saturday morning, his face solemn, that he could not go further in becoming a Catholic. His reasons were simple and compelling. The previous week we had talked about ethics, discussing how it was often just as wrong to allow evil to be done in our presence as it was to commit the acts ourselves. Now he explained to me that it was common on his beat for some cops to accept bribes from local businesses so that the police would look the other way when necessary. While he himself did not participate in that behavior, he felt that if he became a Catholic, he would be compelled to turn in his dishonest comrades, which in turn could lead to serious harm being done to him or his family. His solution was to continue in silence and forgo being baptized a Catholic. I admired his integrity and had no way to counter his reasoning.

Later, though, he called me and set up another meeting. This time he was smiling from ear to ear, because he had figured out a better solution. He would put in for a transfer to another precinct, where for whatever reason such unethical behavior was not occurring. That way he could become a Catholic and not compromise himself or endanger himself or his family. He knew that this move could affect his career on the force. But for him it was still the right thing to do.

Not long after that discussion we celebrated his joyful baptism, followed by another memorable gumbo dinner. It was just as good as that first meal, and I again ate so fast that I had to stick my head out the living room window to cool off my mouth. But the meal wasn't the only reward for me. When my grandmother died later that year, my friend provided a personal police escort from the church to the cemetery. I heard many years later that he had been made a captain, and I could not have been happier for him.

Looking back over the years, I realize that many good things, many graced moments, include a meal along the way. I am glad I took a chance with the gumbo. When I eat a pale version of it now in some restaurant, I remember what that first taste led to. I invite us all to leave the peeled hot dogs to the less adventuresome and take a chance. Who knows where a good bowl of gumbo, or whatever, may lead us?

16

THANKSGIVING CHICKPEAS

*I*t was a dark and stormy night . . . I always wanted to start one of my stories with that line. It fits this story about the Thanksgiving eve when I learned what it really means to show gratitude for God's many gifts to me.

The evening before Thanksgiving started uneventfully. I was going to dinner with a deacon who was soon to be ordained a priest. Trying to avoid the high valet-parking fee charged by the upscale Italian (what else?) restaurant, we drove around for quite a while looking for a parking space. Finally a car pulled out of a spot that was both large enough and legal. The only problem was that it was three blocks from the restaurant.

We were dining at no ordinary, red-sauce-and-meatballs Italian restaurant. The menu was written in Italian, with meager English descriptions of elaborately concocted pasta dishes, veal and seafood, and other items

I confess I could not translate. I broke one of my cardinal rules that night by eating in an Italian restaurant that served pasta costing more than twenty dollars a serving.

After having a drink, antipasto, soup, and salad, all accompanied by crisp bread dipped in seasoned olive oil, I couldn't possibly finish the main course: bow tie pasta cooked with garlic, oil, spinach, and chickpeas. In fact, we declined dessert, and I settled for a double decaf espresso with a lemon twist to settle my stomach before we left. The great conversation and a little red wine had left me feeling very relaxed.

When we walked out the door, a mixture of snow and rain greeted us through a fierce wind. It would not be a pleasant walk to the car, and jogging after eating all that food was out of the question. So we put our heads down, and I held the bag with the leftover pasta close to my side as we set off. Traffic was heavy, and at the first corner we had to wait for the signal to change before we could cross the street. That's when I noticed a street person huddled in a doorway, sitting on the stoop. He was protected from the sleet but certainly not from the cold.

"Hey, guys," he said to us. "Help a hungry guy out?" Did I look that full and now that guilty? I walked over to him and pulled out a five-dollar bill, more to make me feel better than to fill his stomach. But it didn't work. By the time I accepted his sincere thanks and turned away from him, the traffic signal had switched twice, and I was forced to wait again for it to change. My friend had already crossed the street and was closing in on the car. I turned and looked at the man on the stoop once more. I walked back over to him. He looked up, and I asked, "Would you like some pasta?" I realized that I sounded kind of foolish as I handed him the bag from the restaurant, so I started to stammer about how it had chickpeas and I didn't know if he liked chickpeas. Before I knew it, he had not only opened the bag and pulled out a plastic fork from somewhere inside his tattered coat, but he had also exclaimed that chickpeas were one of his favorite foods. Not wanting to stand there and watch him eat, I turned to cross the street. Once again the light flashed red and traffic started flying by, so once again I had to wait. Meanwhile, my friend was at the car, and I had the key.

Then I heard the guy in the doorway call me back over to him. He reached into his coat pocket and pulled out the five-dollar bill I'd given him. "This pasta is great and will be more than enough for me," he said, handing the money back to me. Then he pointed out another street person, standing in a staircase across the street. "Why don't you give him the money? He looks as hungry as I was. Thanks again, man. I can't remember the last time I had chickpeas." I didn't say anything. I didn't know what to say. Now the light was green, so I crossed the street. I walked right up to the guy who had been pointed out to me and handed him the five-dollar bill. He looked surprised, but he took it and thanked me as I walked away. I stopped and turned back to him and said, "Don't thank me. Thank that guy in the doorway across the street." Then I walked toward the car. I'm sure I left him pretty confused but happy to have an unsolicited five-dollar bill in his pocket on a wet, snowy night before Thanksgiving.

I got to the car, and after my friend and I both got in, he asked me what all that was about. I wasn't too sure. I was feeling a lot of things, and not all of them were positive. I found myself saying simply, "Happy Thanksgiving." I think he understood, because we drove back to the rectory in silence.

17

FROM THE OLD
TO THE NEW

*W*hile making a potful of neck bones a while
back, I was struck with an amazing rev-
elation. Sometimes I receive insights while I'm cooking,
because that activity puts me into a zone that is occasionally like the zone I get into when I pray. Usually these
revelations come after I have consumed the pasta and
gnawed the meat from the bones in a sloppy orgy of sauce.
(It tastes better than it sounds. Trust me on this.)

This day, though, the insight came while I was cooking. Or, rather, cheating. I wasn't making the sauce from
scratch, as my mother had done years ago on Saturday
mornings in preparation for Sunday pastas. There was
no way I could match her recipe, which included tomato
paste, canned tomatoes, spices, meats, and more, all slow
cooked for literally hours under her watchful care and
with periodic stirring. I never had that kind of time. So

after years of experimenting, I came up with a passable alternate recipe of which I am quite proud.

I bake the seasoned neck bones in the oven just as Mom did. While they are cooking, I take four or five jars of whatever tomato sauce is on sale, making sure it is a simple marinara sauce with as few additives as possible, and pour them into a pot. I add two cans of diced tomatoes already flavored with garlic and/or basil, three-fourths of a cup of grated Parmesan or Romano cheese for body, and a whole sweet onion. My secret ingredient is a cup of dry red wine. From the nectar of the grape comes the earthiness, the passion, the opera, and the heritage that is tomato sauce. Finally, I add the neck bones, to make the meat tender and to give flavor to the sauce. In a couple of hours—the longer the better—I have a sauce almost worthy of Mom.

I was cooking neck bones on this particular day because I needed comfort. I'd been having what could only generously be called a bad week, or maybe a bad month. My problems were multiplying, and my long hours at work did not make things better. The more I did, the more the parishioners expected of me. They wanted me to take more time for myself—except when they needed me. Then I had to be there. And I contributed to the problem:

I did not say no, I avoided taking days off, I shortened vacations.

My ministry had become reactive, not proactive. I was doing whatever my calendar told me to do and what I could squeeze in between appointments. I had ceased to be creative, in my work and in my life generally.

When my body suffers, so do my psyche and my spirit. I was hurting. I didn't have the time or the energy to start a number of programs that seemed necessary in the parish. There were issues in the larger church that needed to be addressed and questioned. I wanted more time to pray and to reflect and to write. I was unhappy and too tired too much of the time. At least temporarily, tomato sauce would soothe my soul.

I've discovered that, more often than not, God eventually steps in and provides what I need. On this day, God did just that, right when I was testing a neck bone. I remember the moment: the flavor was right, but the meat was not quite tender.

For some reason, my thoughts turned to our parish computer system. (Yes, sometimes my thought processes scare me.) We had hired a computer expert from a neighboring parish to network all our computers and begin linking us to larger systems, and to generally provide us with whatever we needed to function well. As pastor, I knew that I had to work on my own nearly nonexistent computer skills. To me, a "megabyte" was an attempt to swallow a meatball whole. But we were progressing.

Soon I was presented with an opportunity to use technology in a whole new way. A parishioner came to me one day with tears in her eyes. There had been a death in her family, and one of her relatives needed to be comforted, to be told that the beloved deceased was now in the hands of a loving God, not one who throws us into hell. The parishioner asked me to contact her relative and gave me a folded note with all the details on it. I opened it later, expecting a phone number but finding instead an e-mail address.

So for the first time, I used the Internet to comfort someone I had never met. I introduced myself and then shared with the person out there in cyberspace my belief in our loving, forgiving God. The next day, the parishioner showed me the e-mail response she had received from her relative and urged me to check my e-mail. My message, it seemed, had come at just the right time and had said what needed to be said. The mourner was at peace and was grateful to me.

Still, I would have preferred to sit with her face-to-face, maybe even to put my hand in hers. I would have wanted to look her in the eye, or at the very least to hear her voice, so that I could have responded to what I heard in the inflections and the pauses. But e-mail had been my only option. It was a whole new way to minister.

A quick tomato sauce or an electronic message—they really aren't very different. Either will do in a pinch. And sometimes we will be surprised at how good everything turns out. Over a stove and over a keyboard, I am learning, albeit painfully slow sometimes, to do the best I can and to let God's grace and loving presence do the rest.

When I sat down finally over the steaming bowl of pasta and bones, I was satisfied. My life did not magically get better—even the best sauce can't do that (well, maybe Mom's could)—but I did learn that when I lessen my expectations, sometimes God will surprise me enough to get me through a few more days or weeks or months. I can't really ask for more than that, either in my cooking or in my ministry.

18

COOKS,
NOT CHEFS

*O*n a shelf above the stove in my kitchen is a collection of about twenty-five cookbooks. Some are ornate coffee table books. Others are ordinary and functional. Some contain quite complex recipes, and others are obviously geared for the novice. Some specialize in single-pot dishes, while others require all the equipment I have in my kitchen and a lot more besides. A good number of these cookbooks, to no one's surprise, are filled with Italian recipes. I confess that while I page through them occasionally to get an idea or find a solution to a problem, I have rarely followed a recipe completely from beginning to end. That is just not my style.

Sometimes this can prove to be disastrous. Substituting Tabasco for paprika (same color) and cinnamon for nutmeg (I'm hung up on the color thing) and using bananas instead of apples (no excuse here), I created a chicken dish that went beyond interesting to inedible. The idea was to turn the original recipe, with its Danube flair, into more of a Caribbean dish. I quickly learned that some foods don't go together even though they sound as if they could.

I don't know why people say that men make the best chefs. Besides being a blatantly sexist comment, it presupposes that everyone who cooks for others aspires to the title of chef. Not me. I much prefer to be called a cook. And the best cooks I know are women. I think this is because women find it easier to express their emotions, and that expression comes out quite often in their cooking. That's why Italian men can be such good cooks too. They also share so much of themselves in the process of cooking for others: their love of family and God, their need to nurture and heal, and so much more. Let me give you some examples.

One of the best soccer players I ever coached when I taught at Quigley came with his family to Chicago from Poland in the 1980s. His mother had a PhD and was bringing up three sons. She cried when she stepped into a supermarket in the States for the first time, because of all the variety—no longer would she be limited to whatever a state-run store happened to have in stock on a particular day. Now she would have the opportunity to express her love in creative ways that had been impossible before.

My friends Ann and Jim are another example. Both were from New York City—he was as Italian as a pepper-and-egg sandwich during Lent, and she, with her red hair and quick smile, was forever the radiant Irish lass. They fell in love, married, and brought up a family. Ann became an excellent Italian cook. Some would say she did it out of self-preservation. But I know Ann. She did it out of love for Jim and her family. Even today, her family gathers on Wednesday evenings for pasta. And although Jim has died, his presence is still clearly felt. The family helps Ann cook the meal now. I have been just one of many guests who have become part of the family around their table.

A similar story could be told about my aunt Ola, a war bride from Australia who learned Italian recipes from my uncle Frank's family to add to her own baking skills. Her table was always set with love and her meals served with stories and laughter. Uncle Frank was a great cook in his own right. I remember him standing in the backyard in his apron, grinning from ear to ear as he grilled a turkey on a warm Sunday afternoon.

Chefs work with exacting recipes. But cooks work from the heart. They know instinctively when a little more spice is needed and when to hold back on it a bit. Cooks are not good at writing down their recipes. After all, how much is "a pinch or two" really? It comes down to feel and taste rather than design or science.

I have learned this lesson many times. Once, when I was cooking an eight-course dinner for six parishioners who had won the meal in a silent auction, I tried to cook a batch of my mother's tasty egg balls. Instead of turning out golden, light, and fluffy, they were brown and soggy and heavy. When I asked her what I had done wrong, she asked me if I had remembered to use the baking powder? I had not. I asked her how much I should use the next time, and she smiled at me and said, "You'll know." So the next time I tried to conjure up Mom's egg balls, I put in three or four heaping tablespoons of baking powder. Subtlety is not one of my strengths, in life or in cooking.

The first spoonful of batter I put into the hot oil quickly expanded to a football-sized egg ball that could have made it into *The Guinness Book of Records*. Clearly the batter would need a little adjusting before I got it right.

The best way to learn a cook's recipe is to watch the cook. This is what my brothers and I did; we watched Mom. Now when we get together we continue to prepare and eat many of her dishes. Not only do we remember the ingredients and the techniques, but we also recall many family memories at each gathering.

Jesus gave us a way to recall and to share all that he felt for us when he broke bread and told us to do this in his memory, and we have been doing it with very few changes for more than two thousand years. Cooks, good cooks, provide us with a similar way to remember one another.

19

OCCUPATIONAL
HAZARDS

*P*riests get invited into lots of homes, and I think this is a good thing. When we're with people in the comfortable surroundings of their own space, we seem less remote to them and easier to talk to. I couldn't begin to count the homes I have visited over the years. Most of these occasions have involved a meal or at least a cup of coffee and a slice of cake or pie. Regular visits to the matriarch of a longtime parish family have provided me with old-fashioned pineapple upside-down cake—the first piece in her kitchen and the rest packaged for me to take home. I am doubly rewarded: I do my work as a priest, which I enjoy, and I am given something home-made to eat as part of the visit. I can't complain about that, can I?

Actually, I can. We live in an imperfect world, and not everyone cooks like Betty Crocker. There have been times when the meal set before me was a bigger challenge for me than the problems or concerns that brought me into the home in the first place.

There was the family who put sugar on everything before serving it: sugar on the salad, sugar on the green beans, sugar on the mashed potatoes, and even sugar on the roast beef. My plate had a caramelized glaze before, during, and after the meal. Even the ice tea and the coffee were presweetened. It was no wonder that by the time dessert was served (four kinds of ice cream with sugar sprinkles), everyone was talking faster and faster—the sugar had entered our bloodstreams. At least the meal helped me realize why the son was so hyper at school. When I went to bed that night, my teeth were aching and my pulse was racing. I could not bring myself to accept another invitation from them for dinner. It was just too risky.

Another family would invite a group of three or four priests for dinner about four times a year. Two of us would come together in self-defense. We tried to help each other find a reason to leave and not to schedule another dinner because the food was so bad. But one of the other priests would praise everything that was served. I am sure he was most sincere about it, but the rest of us would struggle to find something to enjoy. The salad was always wilted, with barely a trace of dressing. The bread was microwaved to a texture so chewy that one priest actually lost a cap on his tooth biting into a piece. The potatoes were under-cooked, so mashing them must have proved a challenge. And the main course? Suffice it to say that on the drive home after the meal, we were still guessing what kind of meat we had eaten. It was always served with a sauce that was tasteless yet somehow hid the flavor of the meat, so we could never tell if we had eaten beef, lamb, pork, or chicken; we simply referred to it as the "mystery meat."

We endured these meals for a couple of years before the priest who had professed to enjoy them so much stopped coming. Maybe he had been covering up his real feelings, or maybe he knew something we didn't. Finally, one evening as our hostess pressed us to pick a time to join them again for dinner, I blurted out, "We can't keep taking advantage of you like this. Let us take you out for a change. And we won't take no for an answer." We didn't mind paying for a few extra meals at a restaurant if it meant not having to deal with the mystery meat. It will always remain a mystery, and maybe that's a good thing.

When my oldest brother had surgery, I went to Virginia to be with him. While he was recovering in the hospital, the elderly German couple who lived next door to him had me over nightly for dinner. It was their way of showing concern and being helpful, but it almost ended in disaster after the first meal. After all that wonderful Bavarian food—the potato pancakes and the schnitzel and the roast pork cooked by the wife—the husband insisted I try a cup of his homemade yogurt to help me digest the dinner. He had gone back into the kitchen when I tried my first spoonful. Between the sour taste and the slimy texture, it would not go down, no matter how hard I tried to swallow it. It finally ended up in my napkin. The wife chuckled and whispered to me that she hated it too. She took my cup and dumped the yogurt into a potted dieffenbachia, which, judging by its scraggly appearance, had clearly been fed the same stuff before. She then did the same with her own cup of yogurt before her husband returned. This became our ritual for the two weeks I shared dinner with them. One day after my brother came home and just before I left, I saw the plant in their garbage, dead. *That could have been me*, I thought.

There is always a risk when we break bread with others, but the risk goes well beyond the quality and taste of the food. We risk intimacy as well, when we sit at someone's table. We learn a lot about each other. And sometimes we reveal more about ourselves than we intended. It's humorous now to recall the meals that I found hard to get down. But it's also humbling to remember how vulnerable people have become when they have invited me into their homes and prepared food to present to me as a gift. It is something like how vulnerable we become when we offer our own gifts to others and to God. I know how poor my efforts have been on many a day, how others—including the Lord—have likely choked on my words or my feeble attempts to do the right thing. I am so grateful that even when I fail, I am welcomed back again and again.

Is it any wonder that gathering around the table of the Lord, where Jesus asks us to "do this in memory of me," is central to our worship? I know that all too often we don't feel the intimacy we should at a liturgy, because of the heat, the uninspired homily, the poor sound system, or something else. But then there are those times, those special moments, when we feel an intimacy with each other and with Jesus that goes beyond description, and it makes up for all the other meals at the altar that were not what they should have been.

20

HOT DOGS
ON THE STOVE

*D*uring my years at my former parish, I would at times be called to a home that had not been touched by the gentrification that had transformed the surrounding neighborhood. A far cry from the ethnic stronghold it had been years before, now the neighborhood was a place for the wealthy young, and the renovation had raised housing costs to the multimillion-dollar range. A few of the old-timers had stayed and seen it all, and I thought I knew most of them. But one night, a midnight call brought me to a four-story walk-up to anoint a man whose name I did not recognize.

The caller identified himself as the son of the man who needed to be anointed. He was in New York on business, and the paramedics had called him from his parents' home. He gave me the address, not five blocks from the church, with detailed instructions on how to enter the building from the alley and how to walk up the dark staircase. This back way was the only entrance to the two-room apartment.

The old building, surrounded by new and rehabbed single-family homes, was hardly noticeable with its plain, tired-looking facade. The dark, musty staircase confirmed my suspicions that little if any work had been done over the decades to update the building. At the top of the staircase, I knocked on a chipped wooden door that must have been painted a hundred times. An elderly woman with no bottom teeth answered the door in a worn housedress and said, "Hello, Father" before quickly stepping away. I recognized her from Mass, and I'd seen her walking down the street for lunch at the facility for seniors run by the Little Sisters of the Poor. She was a neighbor of the couple.

There were two other people in the room: an elderly woman with yellowed hair wearing a filthy nightshirt, and a man lying in a bed. The bed had been brought into the already crowded kitchen and was beyond dirty. The sheets appeared to have not been changed for months and were curled around what looked more like a mummy than a person. He had been alive and breathing a few hours ago, but now he was dead. His eyes were open, as was his mouth. His gaunt face was covered with sores and scabs and a month's growth of beard. He could not have weighed more than eighty pounds. He was naked, and the sheets barely covered his private parts. Clearly, he had not been cared for. When I tore my gaze from that sad sight and looked over to his wife, I realized that in no way could she have been expected to care for him. I walked past a kitchen table covered with dirty plates and garbage to take her hand and comfort her. She gazed blankly into my eyes. "Talk loud," the neighbor advised. "She can't see and don't hear too good, neither."

As I held the wife's hand, the neighbor told me about how she would bring food to the couple. A nurse had once stopped by regularly, but she had stopped coming. The neighbor had come over that night and had seen that the man wasn't breathing. She called 911, and the paramedics found him dead. They were nice enough to call the banker son in New York. The neighbor's eyebrows went up as she emphasized the word *banker*.

Even though it was winter, the apartment was stiflingly hot. I began to get dizzy but was unwilling to take off my coat, as there was nowhere clean to place it. I wasn't staying long anyway, because the smell of the place nearly gagged me. I figured that I would have to hold my breath so I could do a quick blessing of the body; I justified skipping the full-blown anointing because he was already dead. Before I could do even what I had planned, the neighbor informed me that the son had arranged for the body to be taken to the undertaker after a doctor friend of his arrived to fill out the necessary paperwork. The neighbor's work was done; she would be going back home. There was an outing for seniors the next day that she didn't want to miss. She walked out the door, leaving me alone with the wife and her dead husband and a smell I could not bear.

I stood still for a few seconds to get my bearings. It was then that I realized what was making me sick in the mix of smells—it was coming from the stove. In the middle of all the dirty pots and pans, a dented tin saucepan sat on a lit gas burner. The water in the pan had boiled down to the last few drops, and sitting in it were two bubbled and burst hot dogs. Who knew how long they had been there. I walked over to the stove to turn off the flame. On my way, I stumbled against something and looked down.

On the floor was an old, ornate concertina that had let out a soft moan when I inadvertently kicked it. For the first time the wife turned her head in my direction. She was not as hard of hearing as the neighbor made her out to be. "Don't worry about that old thing," she said. "He won't be playing it anymore." Then she started telling me how as a young man her husband had played it every night in the local bars with different bands and how everyone loved to hear him. I looked over at the bed and suddenly saw not just the corpse I had encountered when I came in, but the shell of a real person who had made music with his life. And I realized that the sightless woman next to me could still see vividly the young steelworker by day and music maker by night who had been her husband for more than half a century. As she talked, I looked at the walls and saw faded photographs of the two of them, much younger, one of him holding the concertina, dressed in his ethnic band outfit.

I felt guilty for having wanted to run out of their home just because it smelled like spoiled hot dogs and because the mess and disarray of death had offended my fragile sensibilities. The wife held my hands tightly as she talked about her husband and their life together. Now I found it easier to stay with her until the doctor arrived. He came in a while later with the paperwork and instructions from the son to bring his mother to a nursing home up the street after taking care of the body. I did a full anointing even though it wasn't necessary. I needed the prayers more than the deceased did, and it brought comfort to the wife. The doctor was good and kind. Clearly, he had assisted them before, so it didn't take much to get her to go with him. I waited until the body had been taken, and then I walked with her to the doctor's car. I assured her I would visit her at the wake, celebrate the funeral, and bring her Holy Communion in the nursing home.

Walking home so late that even the bars were closed—the ones in which all the young people hang out to listen to their music (nary a concertina, I am sure)—I felt fresh guilt. Tonight I had nearly missed meeting two lovely people: one, now dead, who had made music of his own, and one, now blind, who could still see the beauty of life. I had seen only the old, broken people they were on this night, yet they had been active and happy years ago, and in their souls they were still the people they had been back then.

I'm convinced that God saw the music maker and his sighted wife, even as they deteriorated in that crumbling apartment. I think God saw those two hot dogs as an ordinary feast between people who had spent a lifetime together. On that night, I was the one without sight, and I might have stayed that way were it not for tripping over that old concertina.

As I passed one darkened bar on my way back to the church, a sign in the window stopped me cold. It listed the daily specials. Monday was ten-cent wings night. Tuesday was one-dollar longnecks. Wednesday was all-the-spaghetti-you-can-eat night. And Thursday was free hot dogs night. It was now 4:00 a.m. on Friday morning.

Hot dogs—what could be more ironic? Then I noticed another sign, carved into the stone over the entrance to the bar, that read "Established 1933." I wondered if there had been concertina music playing in there way back then, and if the music maker had taken a break to enjoy a hot dog or two with his beautiful wife.

DESSERT

I opened my mouth; he gave me the scroll to eat and said, "Son of man, feed and be satisfied by the scroll I am giving you." I ate it, and it tasted sweet as honey.

EZEKIEL 3:2–3

I dolci means, literally, "the sweets," and Italian **desserts** are legendary. Aside from being sweet and delightful, Italian desserts are also quite personal. No two cooks' tiramisus taste the same. Everyone has his or her own special recipes, as unique as the person who makes them. That is why the dessert after an Italian meal is always an adventure.

Good desserts reflect the sweetness of the time we spend together around the table, as well as the good feelings we will carry home with us when we leave. In Scripture we are told to "taste and see the goodness of the Lord." We have done so at the table, and what we have tasted is sweet. For this we are grateful.

MY OWN LEMON ICE DESSERT

Sometimes people overdress or use too much cologne or laugh a little too loudly. It is possible to have too much of a good thing, and I think that is true about desserts. Sometimes less is more. Italian desserts don't have to be overly sweet. The real sweetness is in all the love that goes into them and that is shared with each and every person around the table.

This dessert goes well with espresso.

INGREDIENTS

1 lemon cake or angel food cake or pound cake, generously sliced

Zest of 1 lemon

Lemon gelato or sorbet

Limoncello liqueur

2 lemons, thinly sliced

Sugar

DIRECTIONS

Place the slices of cake in individual bowls.

Mix the lemon zest in with the gelato or sorbet. Top each slice of cake with a scoop of the gelato or sorbet.

Pour the liqueur over the top of the cake and the gelato (as much or as little as you want).

Dredge the lemon slices with the sugar. Top each dessert with a lemon slice.

Serve immediately.

My Own Macedonia

This is my own version of an Italian dessert made with sweet wine. I leave out the wine so the dessert can be served to children. The fruit needs to be prepared in advance so that it can mix together and marinate, as friends do when they come together for a meal. This recipe calls for bananas, pineapple, blueberries, raspberries, blackberries, and strawberries, but you can use whatever fruits you like or whatever is in season. Serve the dessert in a tall glass with a long spoon. The leftovers are great on breakfast cereal or all by themselves.

INGREDIENTS

5 firm bananas, sliced

1 fresh pineapple, cut into 1-inch chunks, plus pineapple juice

1 pint fresh blueberries

1 pint fresh raspberries

1 pint fresh blackberries

1 pint fresh strawberries, halved or quartered

1 cup sugar

1 cup fresh or bottled lemon juice

1 container Cool Whip

$^{1}/_2$ cup dark chocolate morsels

1 American pound cake, sliced

Italian biscotti

DIRECTIONS

Place the bananas and the pineapple with its juice in a large bowl. Add the blueberries, the raspberries, the blackberries, and the strawberries. Sprinkle the sugar on the mixture.

Add the lemon juice and stir gently but thoroughly.

Place the bowl of fruit in the refrigerator or a cool pantry and stir every half hour. Taste and adjust sweetness with additional sugar or lemon juice.

Just prior to serving, mix the chocolate in with the Cool Whip. Place a small piece of cake on the bottom of each glass. Layer a spoonful of the fruit and syrup on top of the cake, and then add a layer of the Cool Whip mixed with chocolate. Alternate the fruit and Cool Whip layers until you reach the top of the glass, ending with the Cool Whip.

Stick biscotti into the side of the glass and serve.

My Own Mock Spumoni

You won't find chop suey in China or spumoni in Italy. Even though spumoni is not really Italian in origin, I've come up with my own version of it. I've combined the taste of spumoni ice cream with the feel of tartufo, which *is* Italian. Sometimes it is fun to step a bit outside the box. Even as we remember and celebrate the past, it is good to try new things at the end of the meal.

Ingredients

1 pint vanilla ice cream

1 pint cherry ice cream

1 pint chocolate ice cream

1 jar hardening chocolate sauce, such as Magic Shell

1 jar shelled pistachio nuts, crushed

Sprigs of fresh mint

Crème de menthe (optional)

DIRECTIONS

Using a melon scoop, place a ball of each flavor of ice cream in a bowl.

Cover the ice cream with the chocolate sauce. Before it hardens, sprinkle it with the pistachios.

Place the bowls of ice cream in the freezer until the ice cream is hard. Before serving, place a sprig of mint in the center of the ice cream and sprinkle lightly with crème de menthe.

You-Don't-Have-to-Do-It-All Dessert

Some of you may find this easy; others, not so much. When guests ask if they can bring something, let them bring dessert. If no one offers, I offer you the following. And I have done this, I want you to know.

Ingredients

Car or phone or computer

Cash or credit card

Directions

Drive to an Italian bakery (like D'Amato's on Grand Avenue in Chicago) or call one or find one online (Italian cooking magazines list lots of them).

Select great cookies, cannoli, or tiramisu.

Bring them home or have them delivered and serve them with coffee and Sambuca.

Remember "all's well that ends well."

21

THE HONOR GUARD

*T*he more love we share at a meal, the harder it is to end the celebration. But end it we must, so that we can carry the memories and the stories and the love wherever we go, like the leftovers packed for us to take along. We will never forget all that has been shared with us. Our faith tells us there will be more to come on another day.

It wasn't easy for me to leave the parish where I had been pastor for eighteen years. I'd always been aware, in the back of my mind, that one day this would happen, but I refused to believe it. My three extensions beyond the normal two six-year terms had led me to think that maybe I could postpone the end indefinitely. The "term limit" policy of a priest's time in a specific parish was created during a time when there was an abundance of priests. Mandating that a priest could be pastor for only so long gave younger priests the opportunity to become pastors and prevented established priests from building little empires. But today, when there is a shortage of priests, the policy has become more of a tool for the church hierarchy to control the influence of the few priests left, many of whom are dedicated to their parishes and serve them tirelessly. My parish was my home, and the people there knew me as a constant in their lives—as a pastor, a priest, and a friend. But we all knew I was there on borrowed time. That knowledge didn't lessen the hurt when I finally had to make the break.

So there I was, with many unfinished projects and all those wonderful relationships I had formed, facing a farewell liturgy. I decided not to fight a losing battle. Such tactics would only cause greater pain than my leaving quietly, and wasn't I supposed to be a healer? The liturgy would be overseen by a committee formed just for that purpose and headed by the president of the parish council, who happened to be a former student of mine. I rested easy, knowing that my farewell would be a classy, faith-filled, congregation-centered celebration with a fun party, tasty food, and plentiful drink.

I was invited to select hymns that were meaningful to me and to the parish, but beyond that I was left out of the planning—a quick and early lesson on letting go that I would have to return to time and again before my last day at the parish. There were many special moments in the liturgy, but a few of them stand out in my memory:

my giving Holy Communion to everyone in the standing-room-only crowd, the children's chorus singing "Ave Maria," and the parishioners all extending their hands over me and blessing me. I had not expected to be ministered to so powerfully by the people I had served.

But of all the memories that I will carry from this liturgy and that I have been given over the years as pastor, the one that will stand out above the rest is of something that happened at the very beginning of the Mass. I did not know that the adults, teens, children, and babies I had baptized over my years at the parish—more than a thousand people altogether—had been invited to be my honor guard. They would surround me as I processed from the sacristy, down the side aisle, and up the center aisle to the altar to begin celebrating the Eucharist. So many showed up, along with others I had baptized earlier in my ministry, that they formed a human aisle for me to walk through; it reached all the way to the baptismal font and well behind the altar. Each of the people I had baptized proudly wore an identifying blue ribbon. I couldn't simply process as usual; I kissed or hugged or shook hands with or patted on the head each and every one of them. It took a little while, but none of us minded. How fitting that the opening hymn echoed one of the main goals of my pastorate: "All are welcome in this place."

There was the two-month-old I had baptized the Sunday before. There were the twins, now four, born so prematurely that I had baptized them in their home— incidentally, where I also ate some of the best Italian wedding soup I had ever tasted, made by their grandmother. There was Sammy, one of my first baptisms at the parish, now a strapping eighteen-year-old high school graduate whom we had nearly lost in a tragic auto accident four years before. There was Bill and his family. Over the years I had broken the rules, letting his older children make their first communion even though the family wasn't Catholic, but then ultimately baptizing Bill and his wife at the Easter Vigil, and then the younger children who followed. Some of the faces surprised me; I didn't remember baptizing them. Standing there as well were my niece and her baby and my nephew, who was my first baptism, more than three decades before. Now he is a doctor doing research. He sent me a note after the farewell liturgy saying that he hoped he could make as much of an impact on people's lives as I had at the parish.

I am still waiting to see the DVD of the ceremony. I'm sure I missed a lot of what was going on, and to see it all will be a comfort to me now. I am still not sure what exactly I said in my homily; I only remember that everyone stood to applaud. I wanted them to realize that it was their church and that no one could take it away from them. I hoped that they would always be the welcoming community I knew them to be. Of all the events and the projects I was involved with in that church, I now find that what I miss most is celebrating the Eucharist weekly with the people of the parish.

The farewell celebration flowed into the hall after Mass. There was an understated beauty to it, which I later learned was purposeful. The committee wanted the decorations to mirror classical Italy, as I would be visiting the country on my sabbatical after I left the parish. The reception line went on for hours, prompting my brother to reflect on how few people have ever had people wait three hours to talk to them. The image of Santa Claus with the line of waiting children crossed my mind.

The committee did a great job with the party. The finger food was both abundant and tasty, and liquid refreshments flowed all night long. I had taught them well. I wanted to hold on to every embrace, memorize every word, remember every smile and tear, because once it was over I would have to step away and leave room for my successor to do his thing. It all went by much too quickly.

I share these reflections not to brag about my accomplishments or even to boast about that night of celebration. I just want people to know what great joy there is in priestly ministry and how God uses imperfect tools like me to do the work that needs to be done. God made those eighteen years fruitful and joyful and life changing. The people of the parish were more a gift to me, and a grace, than I could possibly have been for them. I want to document how much God has blessed me. And, being human, I also need to capture it in words so I can hold on to it no matter where my ministry leads me in the future.

Even though I never had a chance to taste the food, including the great desserts, that evening was itself like the ending to an exquisite meal, a feast so sweet indeed.

22

SEDUCED IN TUSCANY

*I*t is probably a dream of most everyone of Italian descent to spend even a few of their God-given days in a rustic villa somewhere in the hills of Tuscany, preferably not too far from Florence. After experiencing a week with two of my brothers and their wives in Rome and Venice—a week that included two near accidents in Roman taxis that quite literally took my breath away and vicious crowds in Venice that on numerous occasions nearly pushed me into the Grand Canal—I was looking forward to spending a week in the quiet Tuscan hills.

There I hoped to be able to reflect on the pressing issues in my life that had arisen during my time between pastoral assignments. The Tuscan sights, I thought, would serve as the catalyst I needed to look beyond my past and into a new and exciting future. I felt that St. Peter's Basilica, the Sistine Chapel, Palazzo Grassi, and ebony gondolas were the perfect precursor to solitude in the hills, where I could connect with my roots and find a way to begin my life's journey again. I knew that I was in need of rebirth, or at least a little bit of resurrection.

After dragging our luggage across Venice and waiting an hour for our rental van, in which our baggage and our bodies barely fit, we began our search for La Scalatta, our villa, located outside Montelupo, near Florence. My brothers Tony and Phil sat up front, and their wives, Bonnie and Donna, and I rode in the backseat. The trip to the villa provided a lot of laughter and a few rough moments. My brothers and I unfortunately share a bad trait: when we get uptight about our own limitations, we divert the blame to the supposed incompetence of those around us. The men in our family, me included, need to be loved and to be in control at the same time. This is a volatile combination. Watching my brothers relate in this way to their wives and to other drivers drove me further into a safe, passive role, a strange place in which I am not really comfortable and in which I seldom find myself. Turned into myself in such a deep way, I should have known, as the van strained up the steep dirt road to the villa, that this strange emotional space would also become sacred for me. Even our defensive patterns and our limitations and sinfulness can lead ultimately to the experience of the sacred.

Soon after our arrival, it seemed that everything I had been storing up—all the emotions I had experienced over my recent difficult transitions—came to the front of my thoughts and feelings. We needed to drive into town to the local co-op to purchase food for dinner and break-fast before the next morning's scheduled tour of Siena. After we shopped, the wives went about fixing a simple but elegant dinner of pasta, salad, and fresh bread and cheese. Afterward, out on the patio, one brother struggled to figure out his new digital camera so he could take pic-tures of the beautiful country spread out before us. My other brother was attempting, with similar frustration, to read and return e-mails on his cell phone. I just sat on the veranda. Bonnie had put on a CD of the Three Tenors. Soon I was crying, and I just sat there, writing so that none of them would notice, blindsided by the sudden surge of emotion.

During our stay in Italy, I dreamed nearly every night of past experiences and relationships in my ministry, and each morning I would awaken with a profound and lin-gering sadness. Sometimes the dreams were vivid and dis-turbing and challenged me. Other times they were soft wisps of warm memories, shimmering like the sun rising through the late-summer Tuscan haze.

During the day, sometimes simple sights, sounds, or tastes would hurl me back to a moment in my past, and painfully so. Once I was reminded of Mom when I saw a black scarf with red roses in a shop window—something I would have bought for her. When I touched the scarf, Mom's death returned to me sharply. A multicolored glass box in another shop led me to remember past travels with a friend who collected boxes. Where had that friendship gone? My brother Tony's irritated slap on the back of my head as I got confused over the map and directions reminded me of growing up the youngest and always trying to catch up. How ironic that earlier, over a Venetian dinner, my sister-in-law had asked if I still felt like the little brother. I do in more ways than anyone can understand.

Then, one evening on the veranda, we all stopped what we were doing to look at the sunset. As the sun slipped behind the distant hills, that same sister-in-law remarked that what we were watching must be like what happens when we die. As the last glow of the sun disappeared, leaving violent shades of orange and red in the sky, Luciano Pavarotti was finishing "Nessun Dorma" with the words "Vincerò! Vincerò!" translated "I will win! I will win!" I wanted to tell my family that this was the song I wanted playing when I died. But I couldn't tell them. So I stood there alone, with them. Someday I will share that with someone, maybe the friend who collects boxes and who also loves sunsets.

At that moment, I realized what was happening to me in Tuscany. Like so many others before me, in villas and on hillsides, I was being seduced. And what was seducing me was my own mortality. In the clear absence of intimacy in my life—more specifically, the intimacy of marriage and children—I was facing my own death. What I observed from that veranda was timeless; the view had not changed for centuries. Even the grapevines that crisscrossed the hills were old and gnarled, clinging to the earth for life. In contrast, I was feeling deeply the irreversible passing of time and the impermanence of the things I loved.

My brothers, whom I love dearly, were experiencing this as well, each in his own way. But they were not alone. Each stood next to his wife of decades, deep in the comfort of relationship. As a priest on sabbatical, I would not be going home with or to another, or even to a community of faith in which I would daily break bread.

Although being with my brothers and sisters-in-law made me feel in a fresh way my aloneness as a celibate priest, I realized something else in Tuscany, during the meals we shared together: the one on the shore of the

Tiber River, the one we created as part of the cooking class in an ancient farmhouse, but especially the ones we shared at our villa. I realized that because of my family, I would never be alone. I could always find with them the intimacy I needed. But—and this was the important part—I had to consciously choose that intimacy.

Times of transition are difficult for all of us. We can feel alone, even estranged from loved ones and God. This is when our memories and our stories of the times we gathered to share hospitality, good food, and love become all the more important to us.

While intimacy with others can make us painfully aware of our own mortality, it can also shield us from it. As the darkness of the Tuscan nightfall set in around me, I realized that I had many more dark nights to face. Scripture tells me to leave my mother and father, sister and brother, and follow the Lord. These words now take on meaning I never expected they would. Can I really be ready for what awaits me when the sun rises tomorrow?

23

A VILLAGE
CELEBRATION

*B*esides honoring the holiness of the saints, feast-day celebrations once gave whole towns in Italy the opportunity to stop and celebrate and give thanks to God. In many places, those celebrations are now in the past, perhaps never to be returned to again. But in others, time can seem to stand still, and feast days are still celebrated as they were generations ago.

In the Italian village of Alberobello, the town of my parents and grandparents, the celebration of the feast day of St. Cosmas and St. Damian is not just a one-day event. The actual day in late September is set aside for pilgrims and tourists, who fill the town to overflowing. You can tell these two groups apart: many of the pilgrims go barefoot, while the tourists walk the procession in their Nikes and Reeboks. The narrow streets are almost impassable, especially during the procession. The natives stay home and dine on foods that have been cooking for days, some of it in their little kitchens and some in the large communal ovens that are still in use in such villages. The next day, when all the outsiders have left, the entire celebration is repeated—the Mass, the procession, even the fireworks—for the locals.

But the festivities don't end there. After all the religious aspects are tended to, the celebration shifts into what would be the equivalent of our state or county fairs. For close to a week, rock bands give nightly concerts to entice the young people to attend. The gazebo in the center of the town features bands from around the region, all playing operatic scores while competing for the coveted title of Best of the Feast. This tradition is as old as people can remember. On the first night the town sets up folding chairs around the gazebo. After that, the town collects the chairs, so on subsequent evenings people are forced to bring their own chairs, sit on a curb, or stand. The organizers claim that people steal chairs from the first evening, so they don't want to risk setting them out for another night.

In addition to the music performances, a great marketplace is set up under tents and awnings, with hawkers selling everything from shoes to underwear, CDs to religious articles, electronics to dishes to farm equipment.

You want a watch? You can find a Rolex knockoff for a few dollars or a gold-and-diamond one for hundreds. The scents of candles, laundry soap, perfume, and leather mix in the air and hover over the crowd. Like a flea market gone crazy, the marketplace is full of people arguing about prices, gesturing, and walking away only to spin back around when the seller moans that he is losing money already on the deal. For many, this is a time to shop for necessities that won't be around again for a while and to splurge on some frivolous item that catches their eye.

Further down the configuration of booths, the voices are more muted and the scents more delicate. Here fruits and vegetables both fresh and preserved are expertly and tantalizingly displayed: a melon perfectly sliced open to reveal its juicy innards; mixed nuts artfully cascading out of wicker baskets; cheeses of all sorts, sliced or in whole rounds or floating in water or brine. Cured meats hang from wires, and fresh meats glisten under flattering lights. Barrels overflow with olives, including the disturbingly bright green olives made especially for the feast and said to be cured in lye. As my mother once cautioned, looking at them, *You don't want to be eating a lot of them.*

And for the children there is candy. For this celebration, the candy selection has stretched beyond the traditional honeyed nuts and dried figs that used to be considered treats. Now there is plenty of candy covered with sparkling sugar, more to the taste of today's little ones.

Past the fruit and vegetable stands are prepared-food booths, whose irresistible aromas draw you in. There is no haggling over prices here. You point silently, almost reverently, at what you would like, and then you are so busy eating that there is no time or room for words. My favorite treat is a pizza sandwich. It starts with two pieces of fresh, doughy pizza, each about an inch thick and covered with a light tomato sauce, olive oil, fresh basil, some mozzarella cheese, and who knows what else. Placed between the two slices of pizza are sliced salami and prosciutto and some pickled, roasted peppers. It is almost beyond description. It is best washed down with some of the local wine. And being September, the wine, which is never bottled, is reaching the bottom of the barrel in which it has spent its life. So the white wine is now an amber color and has a deep, nutty taste—a real treat.

Desserts take on many forms, from the creamy gelato that puts American ice cream to shame with its fruity and nutty flavors, to wildly frosted cakes, tarts topped with glazed fruit, powdered cookies, tiramisu, and other lady-finger concoctions. Honey generously covers fried dough or baked nuts. But you won't find spumoni here—despite what some American restaurants claim, that dessert doesn't come from Italy.

In the open space around a corner, a midway is set up with all the latest carnival rides. It doesn't seem to me that the best place to put the carnival is right after all the food booths, but the youngsters seem more than able to handle eating all that good food and then being twirled and twisted and spun and turned upside down under bright, pulsating lights and loud amplified music on rides called American Disco or The Alps. Guys of all ages try to impress not only their wives or girlfriends but also the other guys, buying ticket after ticket to ring the bell or win the stuffed doll that looks enough like Donald Duck to be familiar but not enough to be infringing on a copyright. These festivities continue well into the night.

Throughout this celebration, the church doors are left open. The sounds of the festival seem to drift away as you walk up the stairs to enter the church. The smell of the earlier celebration's incense still hangs in the air. Around the statues of the two saints, in front of rows of melting vigil candles, are bouquet after bouquet of fresh flowers to honor the patrons. Some were bought from one of the booths in the fair down the street. Some were cut carefully and lovingly from a family garden and wrapped with homemade ribbons. If you look closely at some of them, you can see that a picture has been placed in the midst of the blossoms, perhaps of a recently deceased loved one, or maybe a child or a parent in need of the saints' intercession or healing. The saints themselves seem to be looking down at all the flowers with sad, compassionate expressions.

For hundreds of years, the feast-day celebration in Alberobello has been like this, a mix of the sacred and the profane. Elderly ladies clutch their rosary beads and move their lips next to full and tipsy tourists who snap digital pictures so they will be able to remember what the centuries have not forgotten. I know that I am somewhere between the two. I too am overfed, but I kneel to say a prayer.

In the church, I notice the booklet printed for the feast. My family's name is listed under those of the honor guards who pay for the privilege of carrying the statues on their shoulders. I look up at the statues. I know that my parents and grandparents and those before them prayed to these saints. Sometimes their prayers were answered, but even when they weren't, the people's faith didn't waver. This could never be understood by the tourists who have just walked out the door, looking for something else to photograph. The elderly start another rosary. They will pray all through the night. My brief prayer is finished. It is the last night of the celebrations, so before heading back to the hotel, maybe I'll stop for just one more piece of that great pizza. Who knows when, or if, I'll be back this way again.

24

The Art of
Grocery Shopping

*G*oing grocery shopping should feel not like a burden or a chore, but more like that first step in extending our love, and therefore God's love, to others.

I learned this lesson from shopping with my mom. When she was a child, food was never plentiful in her home, a poor household in a small village. As a young girl, she developed Mediterranean anemia and went to live on a farm, where she was exposed to a whole new world of fresh eggs, off-the-vine vegetables, rabbit, pork, and so much more. She learned to appreciate what food could do to strengthen the body, and she also learned the marvelous recipes of the countryside, prepared in the Contadina style of southern Italy, with its subtle use of everyday foodstuffs and its philosophy of sharing abundance with others.

It was her luck to come to America and ultimately marry a man with a grocery store. During the war years, however, the store was not a moneymaking venture. Many commodities were rationed then, and some profit could be made by selling these on the black market, but Dad refused to do that. So Mom was careful in what she brought home from the store to feed her family, especially when that family grew to four always-hungry sons. She never wanted customers or other family members to think our family was literally eating up the profits. At the same time, she could never be seen shopping in a store owned by the competition, such as A&P. Her Friday-afternoon shopping was done quickly and carefully and, I am sure, with no little frustration on her part. The worst-case scenario had me running up the alley to the little corner store where hardly anyone shopped to pick up a loaf of bread or a gallon of milk. When Mom learned that stores such as Goldblatt's often carried bulk items, she would purchase them and store them away, and no one would be the wiser for it.

After Dad retired, he and Mom would go shopping together at the formerly despised competition. Now Mom had to wait for Dad to decide if whatever she needed was a good price. He would pick out cheaper cuts of meats than she would have preferred. It took her a while to train him to think differently. Eventually he understood that unless she had what she needed she could not effectively feed the family, now grown to include daughters-in-law and grandchildren, at Sunday pasta. We kids would make it easier by bringing the dessert or taking everyone out for ice cream after the dishes were done.

As Dad slowed down, one of us would take Mom shopping. But she was always in a rush, because she had to get home quickly to take care of him. In his mellowed old age he would watch us unpack all the bags with a sense of pride that he could still be the provider for his family.

After Dad died and before Mom sold the house, Sunday pasta was still a family tradition. By now, my two Scandinavian sisters-in-law had become excellent Italian cooks and would help Mom with the meal. One of my brothers or I would come to her house during the week for a visit, and we'd ask Mom if she needed to go to the store. She would always preface her affirmative response by asking if it wasn't any bother to take her and assuring us that she needed only a few items. And off we'd go. The few items inevitably became six or eight bags. She always needed to stock up—especially in the winter, in case we couldn't make it to her house to take her shopping. But it became clear to me that late in her life she could finally enjoy buying what she wanted and as much of it as she wanted, and in that way she would always have enough to cook—not for herself, but to share with others.

Our shopping styles weren't necessarily compatible. I liked to shop methodically, up and down each aisle, checking everything out, making sure I didn't forget anything and doing a little bit of impulse buying at the same time. Mom, on the other hand, was a recipe shopper. She knew what she needed for the meals she was planning to fix and would shop meal by meal, which meant a lot of backtracking and walking around today's large supermarkets. Sometimes we would hit the same department, such as canned vegetables, three or four times. She would end her shopping with a list of non-meal-related items that we would split up and hunt down separately. This sort of backtracking and wandering around led to a lot of impulse buying on her part, which she thoroughly enjoyed. Even then, she was shrewd enough to buy, even on sale, only those items she would use.

Our shopping trips continued for a while when she moved into a newly built senior residence. It was odd to smell the aromas of her home cooking wafting down the hallway of what looked like a swank hotel. She always made enough to share with the new friends she made there, so there was still shopping for us to do. As she grew older, she cooked less. More and more, we would go down to the dining room for lunch or dinner. I can't count the number of times she introduced me to the other residents as her priest son and the baby of the family—a 250-pound, gray-bearded baby.

My brother's families kept the tradition of Sunday pasta going, and we promised we would continue it after Mom died. But grandchildren now have children of their own, and people work on Sundays, and Dad and Mom, the glue that held us together, are gone. So our getting together is much less frequent and strangely more special, even as I look back on how joyful all those Sundays with the folks were. Sometimes, truth be told, we'll gather on a Sunday for an all-American barbecue, without a rigatoni or a mostaccioli in sight.

Mom's relationship to food and cooking has left us with a rich inheritance. One of the greatest joys of my life is sharing a meal with friends and family, from the catching up over antipasto to the storytelling and reminiscing over dessert. And now I find myself shopping with wild abandon, as Mom finally was able to do. I have found that shopping is the beginning of a long and beautiful ritual of sharing. Nowhere in this process can there be any holding back or scrimping. From the shopping to the preparation, I feel anticipation for what is to come and profound happiness in making it all happen.

So you'd better watch out for me if you see me in a grocery store. And it would be smart to get out of my way. I'm a man on a mission.

AN ITALIAN KITCHEN

*T*he place you call home might not be the place where you grew up, or even a place where you spend all of your time. It simply has to be a place that is sacred for you. As a priest who had always lived in rectories, I had to learn this concept recently when I moved into my own new home.

During my sixteenth year as pastor at my former parish, my mother died after a long and amazing life. The parishioners had come to know her from her presence at liturgies and parish functions. Many of them had bid on the afghan that she knit every year for the silent auction—each one christened her "last one," only to be overshadowed by one even more beautiful and intricate the next year. Most of all, they had gotten to know her from the stories I told in my homilies about her and my family.

Before she died, Mom moved into a senior residence. It was hard for me to watch her sell the family home and move into her apartment, even though I knew it was the best thing for her. For many priests, who don't marry and start families as their siblings might, our parents' home remains the only home we'll ever know. But to my surprise, Mom's apartment became home simply because she was there. Initially she would cook for me as she always had. As that became more difficult for her, we would go down to the dining room for lunch or dinner. It was hard for me to see how much she had slowed down. We couldn't eat until she was done introducing me as her "baby," the youngest, and as the "priest" son. Long ago I stopped minding those introductions because I saw how genuinely proud she was. Like most of the residents, she brought a large purse in which to gather leftovers to take back up to her apartment. That was why she encouraged me to order more than I could eat, no easy task.

What I enjoyed most about those visits was hearing her stories. For instance, she shared how her brother's fiancé would not let her be in their wedding party because she thought Mom was too fat and would ruin the pictures. Not only did Mom help pay for the wedding, but she also cooked all the food for the reception. After all, her brother was the groom, and nothing and no one should get in the way of family. How could I not treasure stories like that?

When Mom died, the parishioners supported my family and me at the wake and the funeral and during those difficult days right afterward. Still, in the weeks and months that followed her death, I increasingly felt like I was drifting. Without Mom, and without her space to call home, I had no one and no place to anchor me. I knew this was unhealthy and that it would only become worse if I didn't take some positive steps.

This sort of transition is not unusual for priests. At such times, many will purchase a place of their own, a place where they can stay overnight, just to get away from church business and church property, because it can be difficult to "live over the shop." It's a place a priest can call his own, so that he isn't so rootless. Some priests buy these places with money they have saved since ordination, monetary gifts that become a nest egg. But I had used those gifts to pay for my ordination party. My folks had not paid for my brothers' weddings, so I wouldn't let them pay for my reception. Some priests pay for a home with the inheritance they receive after their parents die. But when Mom's estate was settled, there wasn't much to share among her four sons, which was the way we'd wanted it. She had worked hard all her life and deserved to enjoy the fruits of her labors. For my part, I kept lending out what I should have been saving, and often it wasn't repaid—it might not have been good business, but people needed the help at the time.

I would occasionally look for a small place in the city, a high-rise apartment where I could feel at home and to which I could get away when I was able. Everything was beyond my limited means until I found a unit in an old Chicago landmark co-op building. Unlike all the places I had seen that I could not afford, this one instantly felt like home, even with every wall painted pink by the previous owner, now deceased. I stretched myself as far as I could and made an offer, which her family accepted, to my surprise.

With the help of Jim Kelley—a handyman, parishioner, and friend—and others, I fixed up the old place. Some of the parishioners even threw me a housewarming shower, which embarrassed me. But I got dishes and toasters and things every home needs. By their generosity, they were saying that they knew I needed my space and were happy for me.

Of all that I do in my new home—sleep, write, read, pray, watch TV—what I enjoy most is cooking. My kitchen is small. Taking advantage of its old cabinets and wooden floor, I tried to model its look and atmosphere

after an old-fashioned Italian kitchen. I knew I had suc-
ceeded when my niece recently came to visit with her
daughters, Grace and Faith. She walked into the kitchen
and said to me, "Uncle Dominic, it smells just like Nana's
kitchen." That simple sentence brought tears to my eyes.
If it smells like Mom's kitchen, then I must be home.

REFLECTIONS FROM THE ETERNAL CITY

*E*ach of us faces times when we are alone. The kitchen is dark. The table is empty. But even these moments can provide us with the opportunity to remember the good times, the wonderful stories, and the bountiful tables. Those memories can help us through the dark times and support us until we come up on the other side again.

Eighteen years after my first trip to Rome, I returned for a fifth visit to the Eternal City. Every time I have visited the city, the pope has been away from the Vatican. There is a standing joke among my friends and family members that he must have known I was coming. Except for my first visit, when my family and I did what tourists do in Rome—saw the sights, ate fabulous food, and were nearly run over in the busy streets—Rome has just been a transfer point on my travels to the family hometown in the south of Italy. On this latest trip, though, I would be spending some time in Rome before moving on to Venice and ultimately to Tuscany.

My fifth trip to Rome was different in a lot of ways from the trip eighteen years earlier. My knees had a harder time with the cobbled walkways of the piazzas. I needed to join in the afternoon siestas rather than pushing on with the sightseeing. I had a much harder time getting in the smaller cabs. My understanding and knowledge of Italian words had faded more than some of the medieval tapestries we saw in the Vatican museums. And I was truly grateful that the hotel was more American in style and attitude than some pensione; I preferred the comfortable to the quaint. Even so, I wished that the air conditioner would crank out a cooler breeze. And the nine-hour flight there, despite the business-class seating, was uncomfortable. I realize that a lot of the differences were, of course, in me and not in Italy.

Some things, however, had not changed—in me or in Italy. During my first trip to Rome, I had walked through St. Peter's Basilica (joking that I was finally visiting the home office) eighteen years ago and had stumbled upon a small altar at the front right side of the church. It was surrounded by wooden confessionals in which the sacrament of reconciliation was offered in many languages. Beneath the altar and behind glass lay the remains of St. Josaphat, bishop and martyr. Right before that trip I had been appointed pastor of St. Josaphat Parish in Chicago. While I was standing at the altar, as I have related in a previous story, I was approached by an old monk who told me the life story of the saint and urged me to bring the people home to the parish. Even today, I remain convinced that I encountered the ghost of St. Josaphat that day. So on this latest trip back to Rome and St. Peter's, I was eager to say a prayer at the altar and thank St. Josaphat for the good advice he'd given me.

The altar was exactly where I remembered it to be, but for some reason it was roped off. So I contented myself with standing about thirty feet away and saying a brief prayer. My brother, however, told a sympathetic guard that I was a priest, and he immediately let us past the ropes so that I could kneel in front of St. Josaphat for a while. Unfortunately, the old monk was nowhere to be found.

As I knelt there thanking him for my eighteen blessed years at the parish, I realized that, with a lot of help and God's grace, the parishioners and I had made it truly a church to come home to. I knew that my faith had been weak too many times, that at times I had tried to do everything myself, once ending up exhausted and hospitalized.

At other times my faith was tested by those in authority who wanted me to be more concerned about the rules and regulations and less with the needs of the people. I didn't always make the right choices. But in those times I would remember that St. Josaphat had died trying to bring the people together. And that kept me going.

Now, eighteen years after my first visit to the altar honoring St. Josaphat, I had resigned from that parish and was waiting to be assigned to the next. I took these moments before the altar to think about how my pastorate at St. Josaphat Parish had become the benchmark of my life and my ministry. Over those years so much had happened. Mom had died and been buried from St. Josaphat, the church filled with sympathetic parishioners and friends. My three friends in the priesthood—Jim, Jack, and John—who had been with me at my installation as pastor, had also died, each too soon. I felt their presence at my farewell liturgy. Ruby and John—each a spiritual director and friend—also were gone. Like St. Josaphat, all of these loved ones would travel with me wherever my life's journey would lead. I needed to be confident of that.

So, kneeling there in St. Peter's, I had so much to place in prayer. Just as the church had changed dramatically, even as it remained forever the church, I had experienced so much change over the past eighteen years—an ironic realization in the Eternal City. Now I needed the strength and the vision to move on not only to a new assignment but also to a deeper understanding of my priesthood. I left St. Peter's both troubled and at peace, if that is possible.

Later that day, as I sat on the balcony of my hotel room, a small storm passed over the beautiful fall sky. The bright sun on the distant horizon promised that the rain would quickly pass. And so it did. The rainbow that appeared stretched across the sky, touching down at both ends of the horizon. It was perfect. The memory of it still brings me the amazing comfort I experienced at that moment. But as if to give me further assurance, a second rainbow appeared directly over the first, something this city boy had never seen before: a mystical double rainbow. Suddenly I felt at home with myself, and hungry for a great Roman feast. I had been given a sign that brought me a sense of accomplishment and needed closure, a sign that would sustain me and that I carry with me now. This could happen only in the Eternal City.

AFTERWORD

My nephew Mike is an ophthalmologist with three beautiful children. He graduated first in his class at Northwestern University and could have chosen any area of medicine. Every specialty wanted him. He told me that one of the reasons he chose ophthalmology was that it would give him the opportunity to look into people's eyes and so glimpse their souls. If that is the case, he is a healer.

Before he was married and when he was still in school, Mike needed a place to live during one of his summer breaks. He found a job at Loyola University, but housing would eat up a good portion of what he would earn. So I invited Mike to live in the rectory. Between work, going to work out, and being with his future wife, he wasn't around very much those summer months. We'd occasionally run into each other late at night in the rectory kitchen, where we'd sit and chat about whatever was on his mind. The well-stocked refrigerator was one of the perks I think he enjoyed the most. Now he is a healthy eater.

After the summer was over, Mike sent me a thank-you note. It was short, but it took me a while to read; like so many doctors, he had barely legible handwriting. At least we had that in common. In the note he thanked me for the hospitality I had afforded him. And then he told me that it was good to get to know me as more than the uncle who "came home on Sunday, ate pasta, and fell asleep right after the meal was over." It was a pretty accurate description, to say the least.

I hope you have gotten to know me a little better as you've read these stories. You have just finished reading what some might describe as a "different" kind of book. With its reflections, stories, quotes from Scripture, and recipes thrown in for good measure, it might be hard to categorize. I pray that it did not put you to sleep—but I hope it did make you a little hungry. Writing it had that effect on me. In fact, when I was writing about pizza day, I developed a strong taste for pizza, but I was on a roll and didn't want to stop writing. So I went to the freezer and found a small four-cheese frozen pizza, which I quickly threw into the oven. About fifteen minutes later, I had my nose right on the screen of my computer in order to read the words I was typing. They were getting harder and harder to see. Then I looked up, and the entire house was filled with smoke. The smoke alarms started going off as

I ran to the kitchen. I opened the oven door to find, great chef that I am, that I had placed the pizza in the oven upside down. It had thawed, and the four cheeses were melting down the racks of the oven.

Eager to get back to my writing but still hungry, I flipped what was left onto a plate and set the oven to self-clean. No one had taught me that I should have waited for the oven to cool and then wiped up the cheese before letting the oven clean the rest. Within minutes the super-heated oven had turned the cheese into carbon. The smoke I had cleared out by opening all my windows returned worse than before. It took days before my home stopped smelling like the circle in Dante's hell reserved for clergy. I had to put off finishing the story. And I never ate the pizza, my appetite having literally gone up in smoke.

I learned a few lessons from that incident. I learned that the recipes we put together for our lives, even the easiest of them, can be screwed up by our lack of attention to them. I learned that a quick fix can often make matters worse, and that at times we make life so smoky that we have to stop whatever we are doing and just clear the air. And I learned that a little hunger in life is okay.

I hope the words I have written for you have left you a little hungry to find God. Like it has for me, it might help if you share your own stories. Sometimes we don't see where God was with us until we recall the stories of our lives with others. Your stories are waiting to come out of you. And your loved ones may be hungry as well to find where God's love and grace are in their lives. By sharing your stories, you will help them find those special moments. Sure, you could just go out and buy them a copy of this book. (My editors and I are hoping you will do just that.) But your own stories, inspired by the ones you have just read, will be even more special for them.

And do it around the table. If it isn't already, your table will become the most sacred space in your home. Family and friends will gather there eagerly. It makes no difference if you are the greatest of cooks or if you order in—as long as there is more than enough for everyone and it is served with love, and there is time to share stories and to laugh and maybe even cry together, it will be an opportunity to find God's love in your midst.

Then you will realize that your kitchen is not just another room in the house; it is the place from which the love, the concern, the memories, and more emerge. It is a place where you can easily bump into God.

Thank you for letting me share my memories, my stories, my recipes, and my kitchen with you. I hope we can share even more around the table someday soon. We'll share our stories and our recipes and plates of good food from our kitchens. Remember the saying *Il piatto non si restituisce vuoto*. It is an old custom never to return an empty plate. May your plates always be full.